# OLD Stock Market OUT

# NEW Stock Market IN

## Turn the NEW Stock Market Into YOUR Own Money Machine
## 2021-2025

## Take advantage of the NEW Stock Market into which trillions of dollars are being injected

Published by MONEY-PORTAL
©2021 Jacob Nayman
All rights reserved.

*The knowledge and practices in this book are rooted in Nayman's extensive experience-distilling more than 25 years of expertise in his role as a leading investment advisor to the wealthiest.*

# Turn the NEW Stock Market into your own money machine

As a result of the rapid economic and technological changes around the globe, the middle class has become smaller and smaller each year. The end result of this phenomenon is that in the future the world will be divided into two groups of people:

One group with the rich and established, and the other with all the rest.

As the years go by, if you aren't part of the first group you will be part of the second one by default.

Fortunately, it isn't a predestination.
You can become a member of the rich and established by creating your own money machine.

This book will provide you with the necessary knowledge and practical tools to turn the NEW Stock Market into the money machine YOU need to achieve this important goal.

## The Holy Grail of this book
## is to achieve two major goals!

### Your first major goal:

Maximize your profits

in the NEW Stock Market

into which trillions of dollars are being injected.

### Your second major goal:

Protect your money

from possible risks that can pop up

at any given time.

### To meet these two goals:

You will be introduced

to the best and most effective investment strategies

that suit the NEW Stock Market.

# The NEW Stock Market

The thing that most symbolizes the NEW economic and financial reality we are facing today is the injections of trillions of dollars into the financial markets and the economy.

These massive injections are the response of policy makers around the globe (especially in the US) to the disastrous economic impact of the Covid-19 pandemic.

The colossal amounts of money injected into the Stock Market have essentially created a NEW Stock Market.

Most of the investment strategies that were relevant in the past are irrelevant in the NEW Stock Market!

The NEW Stock Market will accompany us for the foreseeable future.

The investment strategies outlined in this book are based on Nayman's extensive knowledge and experience gained over 25 years in his role as a leading investment and economic advisor to the wealthiest.

This book is targeted at investors who wish to invest their money in the US Stock Market, the market in which the largest amounts of money are being injected.

The approach described in this book represents a mindset that can be summarized as

**HOPE FOR THE BEST**

**AND**

**PREPARE FOR THE WORST.**

# Table of contents

# Introduction

The thing that most symbolizes the new economic and financial reality we are facing today is the injection of trillions of dollars into the financial markets and the economy.

These massive injections of money are the response of policy makers around the globe to the disastrous economic impact of the Covid-19 pandemic. The impacts of the pandemic created the danger of a very deep recession - which would be accompanied by disastrous economic and financial effects.

Policy makers around the globe, primarily in the United States, decided to step in and react with the most powerful weapons that exist in their economic arsenal - injection of cash into the Stock Market.

The US Treasury and Federal Reserve began to inject unprecedented amounts of money - trillions of dollars - into the economy and the financial markets, changing the landscape of the stock exchange and creating the NEW Stock Market.

This NEW Stock Market is going to stay with us for the foreseeable future.

Most of the investment strategies that were relevant in the past are irrelevant in the NEW Stock Market!

For you, as an investor, the NEW Stock Market and economic reality present fantastic opportunities - and at the same time, great risks.

The Holy Grail of this book is to achieve two important and major goals:

Your first major goal - Maximizing your profits in the NEW Stock Market, into which trillions of dollars are being injected.

Your second major goal - Protecting your investments from possible dangers, which can pop up at any given time.

In order for you to be able to meet these two major goals, you will be introduced to the best stock investment strategies that suit the NEW Stock Market.

The investment strategies presented in this book will enable you to take advantage of the opportunities created by the NEW Stock Market, while protecting your money from possible unforeseeable risks.

As a senior financial advisor in the banking system and an investment portfolio manager in the private sector, I have met thousands of people from many different walks of life.

While these people were very talented people in their specific fields, they generally lacked any knowledge (even basic knowledge) in the field of financial investments, especially in the Stock Market.

When speaking with layman investors about their financial investments and investing money in the Stock Market, I used a language that is simple and clear, without glossing over the deeper implications the investment information conveyed. This book has been written along this principle, and is designed for investors who lack an in-depth understanding of the field.

The approach described in this book represents a mindset that can be summarized as:

## HOPE FOR THE BEST
## AND
## PREPARE FOR THE WORST.

Yours,

Jacob Nayman

# Chapter 1

## NEW Stock Market - IN
## OLD Stock Market - OUT

### "To Boldly Go Where
### No One Has Gone Before"

This famous Star Trek quote pretty well sums up the new economic and financial reality we are facing today.

What most symbolizes the NEW economic and financial reality we are facing today is the injection of trillions of dollars into financial markets and the economy.

These massive injections are the response of policy makers to the disastrous economic impact of the Covid-19 pandemic, and have created the NEW Stock Market.

Most of the investment strategies that were relevant in the past are irrelevant in the NEW Stock Market!

The NEW Stock Market will accompany us for the foreseeable future.

**BE AWARE!**
This book is targeted to investors who wish to invest their money in the US Stock Market, the market in which the largest amounts of money are being injected.

## The golden rule of the senior investment advisor

Years ago, when I was working as an investment advisor in the banking system, a senior investment advisor with over 30 years of professional experience approached me and asked me to do her a favor.

She gave me the details of her bank account, and asked me to buy stocks for her by purchasing an index/ETF that represented the 500 leading companies in the Stock Market.

Her golden rule for investment decisions was that if the Stock Market went down considerably, she would buy the index/ETF of the 500 stocks, and when, after days or weeks, the Stock Market prices went up considerably, she would sell the index/ETF on the 500 stocks and materialize her short-term profits.

After having materialized her profits, she waited patiently for a drop in Stock Market prices. Once the prices had decreased considerably, she bought the index/ETF again.

Over time, she also gave me the bank accounts of her mother and daughter and asked me to do the same for them.

I used this Golden Rule for buying and selling stocks for the senior investment advisor and her family over five years, and noticed that it produced very profitable results.

## THE GOLDEN RULE (THE SHORT-TERM PROFITS STRATEGY)

Buy stocks (using an ETF) when their prices drop considerably

Sell the stocks (the ETF) when their prices rise considerably

## An ETF

An exchange-traded fund is a type of an investment fund. ETFs involve a collection of securities - such as stocks - that often track an underlying index, although they can invest in any number of industry sectors and can use various strategies.

**BE AWARE!**

*ETFs are similar to mutual funds in many ways, except that ETFs are bought and sold throughout the day on stock exchanges while mutual funds are bought and sold based on their price at the day's end.*

The golden rule used by the senior investment advisor years ago has become very relevant to our current NEW Stock Market.

**The current NEW Stock Market incorporates three conditions that make the short-term profit strategy a winning investment strategy.**

## The NEW Stock Market

If needed, American policy-makers (the Federal Reserve and US Treasury), inject billions and even trillions of dollars to support the economy and the financial markets.

## The short-term (less than a year) profits strategy

Buy an index/ETF on major stocks that have gone down considerably, and sell the index/ETF after a considerable rise in its stock prices.

**IN MY EXPERIENCE**
*The short-time profits strategy is used frequently by leading hedge funds and investment banks.*

There are three conditions that exist in the NEW Stock Market which justify and support the short-term profit strategy.

# Condition number 1
## The "Safety Net" condition

When you invest money in the NEW Stock Market you can be certain that the most powerful economic forces in the world will support the Stock Market if needed. These powerful economic forces are the American Federal Reserve and the US Treasury.

The investors in the market know that if something bad happens to the economy or the financial markets, policy makers will intervene. The policy makers do so by injecting tremendous amounts of money into the economy and the financial markets.

# Condition number 2
## The lack of attractive alternatives to the Stock Market

The major traditional alternatives to investing in stocks is investing in bonds or treasury notes. However, the interest rates that the treasury notes offer and the yields on bonds are currently near zero and even negative.

In contrast, the Stock Market (even if riskier) can produce positive returns. In such an environment, the Stock Market becomes the most attractive investment for investors compared to other financial alternatives.

# Condition number 3

## Rapid rotation of positive sentiment between sectors

If you track Stock Market data over years, an interesting phenomenon becomes apparent - after the value of a specific sector (let's say the technological sector) picks a positive sentiment, and its prices rise to new records, investors have a tendency to look for other sectors that may have been relatively undervalued by investors, whose prices are relatively attractive and more reasonable for purchasing (for example the bank sector).

This phenomenon, in which the "undervalued sector" becomes the preferred sector, is referred to as the rapid rotation of positive sentiment between sectors.

*IN MY EXPERIENCE*
*In normal times, the rotation of positive sentiment between sectors could take an average of three months.*
*In the NEW Stock Market, the rotation between sectors can happen in a matter of only weeks and sometimes even days.*

The third assumption gives us, as investors, the ability to produce **alpha returns** on our financial investment. It also supports the strategy of practicing short-term profits.

## Alpha returns

The alpha of an investment is the excess return of that investment relative to the return of a benchmark index. For example, if the S&P index rises by three precent in one month but you invested your money in the technology sector, which rose seven precent the same period of time, your investment in the Nasdaq sector created an alpha of four precent.

**BE AWARE!**
*If you decide to act in accordance with the short-term strategy, you must be aware of the three conditions and make sure that all of them exist.*

## The short-term strategy as part of an investment portfolio

The short-term investment strategy can be used as a standalone strategy, especially if you have only thousands of dollars at your disposal for investment in the Stock Market. However, it can also be used at the risky and active part of an investment portfolio when you have a considerable sum of money that you want to manage financially. In later chapters, detailed explanations of the rationale will be provided, and a possible portfolio that suits the NEW Stock Market presented.

## A quick snapshot of a possible portfolio that suits the NEW Stock Market:

### The risky part of investments
Short-term profits - using ETFs

### Equity diversification
Invest some of the money in foreign Stock Markets

### Currency diversification
Invest in other leading currencies in addition to the US dollar - such the euro, swiss franc, etc.

### The solid part of investments
Gold, crude oil, linked bonds
Equity and currency diversification
High level of liquidity (cash and equivalents)

## What's next?

In the next chapter I'll introduce you to the mindset you should have, as an investor, regarding the three conditions that justify the short-term profits strategy.

**Conclusions concerning
your investment decisions**

### IN: NEW Stock Market

The Golden Rule of the senior investment advisor
Buy stocks (using an ETF) when their prices drop considerably.
Sell the stocks (the ETF) when their prices rise considerably.

### OUT: OLD Stock Market

Long-term investing.

# Chapter 2

## The Fear of Missing Out - IN
## Sitting on the sidelines - OUT

The massive injections of money into the economy and the financial markets is the response of policy makers to the disastrous economic impact of the Covid-19 pandemic, which includes high unemployment rates, a shrinking GDP (gross domestic product, or national "economic cake"), and low profitability of firms.

The injections of trillions of dollars into the economy and the financial markets have created the NEW Stock Market.

The conditions that make the NEW Stock Market a good place for implementing the strategy of short-term profits is going to stay with us for years ahead.

# The NEW Stock Market matrix

There are three conditions whose existence in the NEW Stock Market justify the short-term profits strategy.

## Matrix - Definition

A set of related entities that affect the way in which something develops or changes.

## Policy makers

The policy makers in the United States are the Federal Reserve and the US Treasury. These entities are considered the leading economic forces in the world.

# The three conditions that justify the strategy of short-term profits

## Condition number 1
## The "Safety Net" condition

When you invest money in the NEW Stock Market you know that the most powerful economic forces in the world - the Federal Reserve and the US Treasury - support the Stock Market.

Market investors know that even if something bad

happens to the economy or the financial markets, policy makers will intervene.

The policy makers intervene by injecting tremendous amounts of money into the economy and the financial markets.

> **ZOOM-IN**
> **Investor mindset**
> When an investor buys stocks in the NEW Stock Market, he knows that the risk he takes is less than the risk inherent in investing in a Stock Market that isn't supported by injections of money. When he invests his money to buy stocks, he believes that the probability that his money will be exposed to sharp and dramatic declines in stock prices is less likely.

## The positive implications of the safety net condition

The investors in the market assume that if anything bad happens, i.e., if there are negative developments in the real economy or the Stock Market, then the policy makers (the American Federal Reserve and the US Treasury) will intervene.

Even in a scenario in which the decline in stocks prices is considerable, it will be reasonable to assume that when the policy makers exercise their decision to support the market and inject money, after a brief delay, we, as investors will see a positive sentiment in stock prices.

The intervention by the policy makers may take time, but in the end, it will happen - and conditions in the Stock Market will improve.

## AN EXAMPLE

If unemployment rates rise significantly (above the expected rate), and as a result, the consumption of goods and services shrinks, chances are high that stocks in sectors directly related to the real economy - such as the banking and automotive sectors - will be negatively impacted.

In the situation described, investors assume that policy makers will intervene and give more money to householders and business owners to spend, in order to increase their buying power.

The injections of money by the policy makers will lead to increased consumption of goods and services by householders and business owners. As a result, stocks that are related to the real economy will enjoy a positive sentiment and their prices will rise.

It may take time for the effects of this kind of intervention to be felt, but the investors assume it will happen in the foreseeable future, and that, as described, things in the economy and the Stock Market will then change for the better.

This powerful assumption and the actual existence of the "Safety Net" condition give the investors the feeling that the Stock Market is a less risky place to invest their money.

**BE AWARE!**
*The assumption of the "Safety Net" condition does not protect investors in the Stock Market from falls of five percent, 10 precent and even more in stock prices.*

## Condition number 2
### The lack of attractive alternatives

When you decide to invest your available money in the Stock Market, you will naturally compare this option to other investment alternatives. If these alternatives are attractive, then you will probably consider investing some of your money in these alternatives as well. But condition number two assumes that there is a lack of attractive investment alternatives to the Stock Market.

# The impact of the lack of attractive investment alternatives

The major traditional investment alternative to investing in stocks is investing in bonds or treasury bills/notes. However, the interest rates on treasury notes and the yields on bonds are near zero and even negative. In such an environment, the Stock Market becomes the most attractive investment for investors: although it is riskier, it offers the possibility of positive returns.

After cashing in and selling stocks to materialize their profits, investors will most likely reinvest this money in the Stock Market.

## The second condition relies on two assumptions:

The first assumption: Low and even negative interest rates on treasury bills and yields on bonds.

The second assumption: The inflation genie is still "in the bottle" and is not yet apparent.

The lack of attractive alternatives explains why it's only a matter of time that prices will rebound after the stock market goes considerably down.

27

**ZOOM-IN**
*Investor mindset*
*When investors have liquid assets at their disposal or cash in from the Stock Market, the big question they ask themselves is where to invest or reinvest this money, if at all.*
*In a financial environment that offers no attractive investment other than the Stock Market, investors will usually choose to reinvest their money in the Stock Market - simply because the other investment alternatives are not attractive enough.*

# The alternatives to the Stock Market are suffering from very low interest rates and yields

If we assume that the interest rates on safe treasury notes are near zero or even negative, and that the yields on bonds are slim and close to zero, then our motivation as investors to invest in these channels (as an alternative to the Stock Market) is also close to zero.

*IN MY EXPERIENCE*

*In a financial environment in which interest rates and yields on bonds are near zero or negative, most investors will prefer to take some of their money and expose it to the risks of the Stock Market in order to get positive meaningful returns.*

## Let's look at an opposite scenario - in which interest rates and yields are high

If we assume an environment in which interest rates and bond yields are high, then the Stock Market becomes a less attractive investment alternative.

For example, if investors can enjoy an annual yield of 5 precent on a government bond, then their motivation to invest money in this safe channel will be greater than if they were offered an annual yield of only 0.5 percent.

# What will happen if the inflation genie appears?

In this scenario, the main investor concern will be to preserve the value of the money invested. In such a situation, investment alternatives other than the Stock Market can be more attractive for investors.

# Products that provide protection from the inflation genie

If the inflation genie appears, other investment channels will become more attractive.

In an inflationary economic environment, the goal of most investors will change from the desire to profit to the desire to preserve the value of their money.

If, for example, the annual inflation rate is 10 precent then channels such as linked bonds (that protect against inflation), commodities such as gold and black gold, and other products such as real estate can become more attractive than simply investing money in the Stock Market.

If there is high inflation or high interest rates, then investing in channels other than the Stock Market also becomes an attractive alternative.

An inflationary reality will negatively impact the prices in the Stock Market.

*IN MY EXPERIENCE*

*When investors cash in to materialize their profits in the Stock Market in an economic environment characterized by no meaningful inflation and very*  *low interest rates, we can assume that most of the money that was cashed in will be reinvested in the Stock Market in the foreseeable future - and that it will happen sooner than later.*

## Condition number 3
### Rapid rotation of positive sentiment between sectors

In normal times, the rotation of positive sentiment between sectors can take an average of three months. In the NEW Stock Market, the rotation between sectors can happen in a matter of only weeks and sometimes even days.

**ZOOM-IN**
*Investor mindset*
*When stocks are at their peak, and after a considerable positive rally in price, investors feel that the positive sentiment has run its course, so they look for other alternatives. In this kind of investor mindset, the probability of a downturn in stocks whose prices have risen considerably is higher than the continuation of the rise in value.*

## The impacts of rapid rotation

If an investor buys stocks in a sector that experienced a considerable downfall and waits enough time, after a while the other investors will rediscover the attractiveness of the sector (because of its low prices of shares). This rediscovery process will impact the sector stocks in a positive way.

*All three conditions justify the short-term strategy.*

## IN MY EXPERIENCE

*If you track Stock Market data over years, an interesting phenomenon becomes apparent - after the value of a specific sector experiences a rise in prices and its share prices reach new records, investors have a tendency to look for* 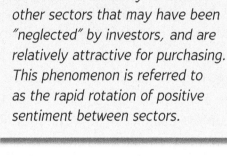 *other sectors that may have been "neglected" by investors, and are relatively attractive for purchasing. This phenomenon is referred to as the rapid rotation of positive sentiment between sectors.*

# FOMO - The fear of missing out

As an investor, your strategy can be "sitting on the sidelines" until the sky in the real economy and the financial markets clears. This period can take years - and you, like most investors, probably have a fear of missing out.

There are many risks in the NEW Stock Market, but there are great opportunities as well. The solution, therefore, is to adapt your investments to the conditions of the NEW Stock Market.

In the coming years there is a high probability that policy makers will continue to support the economy and the Stock Market by continuing to inject money.

Thus, the policy makers will enable investors in the NEW Stock Market to assume and act upon the assumption that the government, using the Treasury and the Federal Reserve, will continue to intervene (if needed) and inject additional trillions of dollars.

The investors in the Stock Market will know there is a kind of safety net that, in a sense, protects their money from a collapse in stock prices - even if the economic conditions continue to be weak or even worsen.

## Summary of the NEW Stock Market matrix

### The "Safety Net" assumption/condition

If needed, the American Federal Reserve and the US Treasury (the most powerful economic forces in the world) will intervene and support the US economy and the US Stock Market.

The "Safety Net" condition - reduces the risk of buying stocks. The risk investors expose their money to is less than the risk in a Stock Market that is not supported by policy makers.

**ZOOM-IN**
**Investor mindset**
In the NEW Stock Market, investors believe that they are exposed to less risk because the most powerful forces in the economic world support the economy and the Stock Market.

## The "Lack of Attractive Alternatives" assumption/condition

Investors prefer to invest or reinvest their money in stocks because the other alternatives are not attractive enough.

The lack of attractive alternatives - explains why it's only a matter of time that prices will rebound after the Stock Market goes considerably down.

## The "Rapid Rotation of Positive Sentiment Between Sectors" assumption/condition

Investors in the NEW Stock Market decide, sooner rather than later, that a sector has run its course. So, they invest their money in another sector that is considered to be undervalued.

The rapid rotation between sectors gives you, as an investor, the justification for buying an ETF on the "unfavorable" sector or index after a considerable fall in its prices. It also explains why, after a large rise in a specific sector, it's time to cash in. You should materialize your profits and not wait for further rises in share prices.

The third assumption gives us, as investors, the ability to produce alpha returns on our financial investment.

## What's next?

Chapter 3 describes all of the various scenarios possible and how investors can prepare for them.

## Conclusions concerning your investment decisions

### IN: NEW Stock Market

**The price of a stock reflects:**

The "Safety Net" assumption.
The "Lack of Attractive Alternatives" assumption.
The "Rapid Rotation Between Sectors" assumption.

**FOMO: The fear of missing out**

As investors, we can wait for the economy to heal completely, and only then invest our money in the Stock Market. However, it may take years before the economy is 100 percent healthy. And most investors won't wait due to the fear of missing out.

### OUT: OLD Stock Market

The price of a stock reflects a company's current value and it also reflects the prospects for a company, the growth that investors expect of the company in the future.

37

# Chapter 3

## Hope for the best - IN
## FOMO - IN
## Prepare for the worst - IN

The injections of trillions of dollars into the economy and the financial markets by policy makers creates an unprecedented gap between the condition of the real economy and the prices of the financial assets in the Stock Market. This gap cannot be maintained forever. There are three scenarios describing how the gap will eventually be closed/resolved.

## The first scenario - the optimistic one: the least likely

The economy will recover quickly and strongly, with a V-shaped recovery. The GDP grows at a rapid pace, unemployment is low, and company (firm) profitability is higher than ever. If all these amazing things happen, then the good health of the real economy and the high firm profitability will justify the high equity market prices - and the gap will be reconciled.

## The second scenario - the realistic one: a period of FOMO + hope for the best

The economic recovery will be slow - a U-shaped recovery. Policy makers will continue to print money and support the economy and the financial markets. Because the economic recovery can take years, the injections of money may lead to inflation pressures. High inflation can bring the worth of the real economy closer to the worth of the equity market - and reconcile the gap.

## The third scenario - the doomsday scenario. prepare for the worst: unlikely in the near future

An "L-shaped" recovery: the economy enters a deep recession lasting many years following additional negative external and internal economic events.

Policy makers will continue printing money until the real economy "gets back on its feet." In this scenario we will experience stagflation - hyperinflation and recession: the equity market will collapse and the new prices will reflect the gloomy state of the real economy.

## The intermediate period - the FOMO period

The existence of the Safety Net condition is assumed because in the foreseeable future, policy makers will continue to print money in response to a slow economic recovery, which will take several years.

In the meantime (until the genie of inflation appears), policy makers will keep injecting trillions of dollars into the economy and the financial markets. These money injections will give Stock Market investors the presumption of a Safety Net condition that protects them from significant losses, even in an economy that is not entirely healthy.

As an investor, FOMO (the fear of missing out) can lead you to invest some of your money in stocks. You can decide to take advantage of the NEW Stock Market by implementing the short-term profit strategy, investing in an index or sector using an ETF.

## Hope for the best - prepare your investments for the worst

You can't control what happens in the economy or the financial markets, but you do have full control over what happens in your private investments (portfolio).

# The level of risk in your investments (portfolio) doesn't have to reflect the level of risk in the financial markets

You can divide your money investments into a risky category and a solid category. In the risky category, build an investment portfolio that exposes some of the money to the Stock Market: these investments will enjoy the injections of money made by policy makers.

The solid part of your investments will protect your investment portfolio if inflation pops up or the economy and financial markets collapse.

## The dilemma faced by policy makers

When policy makers encounter inflation pressures, or when currency problems appear on the horizon, they will face a complex dilemma.

### Option 1

Despite mounting inflation pressures, policy makers will choose to continue to print money, with a tremendous price tag waiting down the road - high inflation and possibly even the considerable danger of losing the global currency status enjoyed by the US.

## Option 2

Policy makers slow or completely stop the injections of money in order to stop the developing inflation. As a result of this decision, the recession worsens - more unemployed, further contraction of the GDP, and the collapse of the Stock Market.

## Explanation

The most important economic asset of the US economy is its currency, which enjoys a very prestigious global status. This status gives US policy makers tremendous economic powers/advantages. If the US loses its currency status, the economic reality, including the Stock Market, will suffer a significant impact.

In both possible future scenarios, you, as an investor, have to protect your solid and non-solid assets from the dangers of each possible event.

## Warning!

The securities and investment strategies mentioned in this book do not constitute suggestions or any type of recommendation regarding what you should or should not invest in. It is highly recommended that if you are not an experienced investor you build and accompany your investment decisions with the help and guidance of a licensed financial advisor.

# A possible portfolio that suits the NEW Stock Market

To protect your money from inflation and maintain your buying power of goods and services, you can consider investing in ETFs such as:

## Commodities

Gold, crude oil

## Linked bonds

Linked government bonds
Linked corporate bonds

# Bonds

The central bank is also a player: it buys corporate bonds, especially if there is a considerable drop in prices or sellout of these securities when times are tough and the volatility of the markets increases.

As a result of the policy maker interventions, the yields/returns on bonds are near zero or even negative.

**BE AWARE!**
*You, as an investor, know in advance that they are not an attractive investment. But if we assume that inflation will pop-up in the future, then linked bonds can be considered a better option than nominal bonds.*

## The index of gold

The prices of gold can be considered a canary in the coal mine, used by miners as an alarm. When gold rises significantly, it may indicate that inflation or currency problems are developing.

In times of inflation, gold can used as a safe haven that protects our money in two ways. First, as a kind of x-ray vision, letting us know what investors think about the dollar and the economy: what we look at is the direction, over time, of the trend in the prices of gold. Second, gold can serve as an investment that protects our money from currency problems and inflation.

To protect your money from a doomsday scenario in which policy makers continue the injections of money (before the economy recovers) but the recession worsens because of additional negative economic events, leading to stagflation, you should consider the following steps:

## High liquidity

Cash and equivalents.

## Currency diversification

Invest in leading currencies other than the US dollar - such as the euro, Swiss franc, etc.

## Equity diversification

Invest some of the money in foreign Stock Markets.

# Equity and currency diversification

The economic challenges that your country faces don't have to be reflected in the risk in your investment portfolio. For various reasons, the economic recovery in different countries may differ from the recovery in the US; therefore, also investing some of your money in their Stock Markets can create an investment portfolio with global diversification, potentially enabling less risk and more profit.

## Currency diversification between countries

If, for example, you believe that there is a possibility that the economic recovery in Europe will be faster than in the US, this means that their ability to reduce their dependency on printing money is greater than that of the US: as a result, their currency can be stronger than the US dollar.

## High liquidity

High liquidity means holding more cash and money equivalents. This is preferred for 2 reasons: first, exposure to the volatility of the financial markets is reduced. By maintaining high liquidity, you create a reality in which your portfolio risk (the risk your money investments are under) is unrelated to the risk in the financial markets. Second, high liquidity means you hold a large amount of cash and its equivalents - giving

**BE AWARE!**
*You - and only you - have full control over how much money to invest (if at all), when to take risks, and how much risk to take.*

you the possibility of exploiting opportunities when the market goes down.

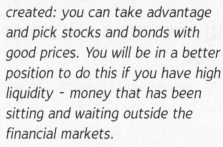

**IN MY EXPERIENCE**
*When there is a major crisis in the financial markets and the prices of stocks and bonds reach bottom / unprecedented lows, opportunities are created: you can take advantage and pick stocks and bonds with good prices. You will be in a better position to do this if you have high liquidity - money that has been sitting and waiting outside the financial markets.*

**The defensive aspect** - When our money is less exposed to the financial markets, we will lose less if the markets fall.

**The offensive aspect** - When the markets fall considerably - liquidity gives us the ability to exploit opportunities and buy stocks at a very attractive prices, using ETFs.

## You - and only you - control your exposure to the Stock Market

You can decide to have zero exposure to the Stock Market, or you can decide to risk some of your money in order to take advantage of the NEW Stock Market into which policymakers are injecting money.

# YOU ARE LIKE A PASSENGER ON A TRAIN

The risk to your money doesn't have to be the same as the overall risks of the Stock Market:

You are like a passenger on a train. You're not the driver, who has to stay on the train for the whole journey.

You decide when to get on - when to buy stocks, how much to buy - and when to get off - when to sell them and profit.

## What's next?

In Chapter 4 you will be introduced to the economic Matrix and see in what economic scenarios the three conditions that support the short-term investment strategy will be maintained.

# Conclusions concerning your investment decisions

## *IN: NEW Stock Market*

### The risky part of investments
Short-term profits - using ETFs

### Equity diversification
Invest some of the money in foreign Stock Markets

### Currency diversification
Invest in leading currencies other than the US dollar - such as the euro, Swiss franc, etc.

### The solid part of investments
Gold, crude oil, linked bonds
Equity and currency diversification
High liquidity (cash and equivalents)

# Chapter 4

## The Economic Matrix - IN Long-Term Investments - OUT

In the previous chapters, the NEW Stock Market matrix was presented and the practical ways of using the matrix to maximize profits were explained. The NEW Stock Market matrix is based on three important conditions.

The current economic reality and injections of trillions of dollars into the economy and the financial markets have created an environment that supports the existence of the three conditions. The three conditions justify the short-term profit strategy.

The short-term investment strategy is based on a simple principle - buying stocks (using an ETF) when prices go down considerably, and selling the stocks (the ETF) and materializing profits when the shares` prices go up considerably.

The important question that we, as investors, must

ask ourselves is, in what kind of economic environment will these three conditions of the NEW stock-market matrix continue to exist?

It is important that you, as an investor in the NEW Stock Market, know the economic metrics of the possible scenarios and their outcomes when making decisions regarding buying or selling stocks in the equity market.

**BE AWARE!**
*The economic matrix that will be introduced will present three economic scenarios that we as investors in the stock-market have to consider. The first two scenarios support the existence of the three conditions. The third scenario does not support the three conditions.*

The economic matrix supports the claim that in the NEW Stock Market the strategy of long-term stock investments can lead us, as investors in the Stock Market, to poor decisions.

## The Economic Matrix

# The first scenario - the optimistic scenario:
## A "V-shaped" recovery
### *A very strong and rapid economic recovery.*

The real economy will recover very fast - resulting in low unemployment rates, a fast-growing GDP, and rapidly rising company profitability.

In such a scenario, the rapid economic recovery will lead to high firm profitability. This high profitability, and even expectations of high profitability (because of the good economic data), will completely justify the high prices that exist in the Stock Market.

When this rapid economic recovery happens, the gap between the real economy and the high prices of stocks will be reconciled.

If the optimistic scenario materializes, it is reasonable to assume that all three conditions will continue to exist:

**The Safety Net condition** - will continue to exist because, if here and there manageable economic troubles pop-up, the Federal Reserve and the US Treasury will help.

**The lack of attractive alternatives** - will still be a factor. The rapid economic recovery will not impact policy maker motivation to support the economy and the Stock Market if needed. However, because the economy will be healthy most of the time, they will inject money less frequently: they will still intervene, but more rarely. Since less money will be printed, the probability of mega-inflation will become very low. Therefore, the Stock Market will continue to be the best investment alternative.

**The rapid (positive sentiment) rotation between sectors** will continue because the Stock Market prices will be at peak levels. After the stock prices in a specific sector rally, investors will look for a different, undervalued sector in which to reinvest their money - and the positive sentiment will move to the new, undervalued sector.

# The second scenario - The realistic scenario:

## A "U-shaped" recovery

*A slow economic recovery that will take between four and five years*

## The medium time frame is more likely

Because of the slow economic recovery, the continued injection of trillions of dollars to support the economy and the financial markets by policy makers will be justified. Policy makers will continue to support the economy until it is healthy enough to stand on its own.

If, after four or five years, the economy fully recovers, this will probably have a positive effect on the firm's profitability in the Stock Market, leading to closure/reconcilement of the gap between the high prices in the Stock Market and the condition of the real economy.

During the period of the slow recovery, assuming the inflation genie doesn't pop up and no major unexpected economic crisis sweeps over the world, it's very reasonable to assume that all three assumptions will continue to exist.

**BE AWARE!**
*At any given moment during the U-shaped recovery, powerful forces, external or internal, can pop up and impact the market in a bad way - jolting the economy from a U-shaped recovery to a deep L-shaped recession.*

# The third scenario - The doomsday scenario:

## A deep "L-shaped" recession

*The economy enters a deep recession from which it takes many years to recover.*

## This is the more likely long-term scenario

Under the effects of additional internal and external economic negative forces worldwide, the real economy won't be healthy even five years from now.

The recession will continue, and the government will continue to support the economy and the market by printing money.

In this scenario (after four to five years of money injections) the probability that the injections of money will create inflation is very high.

# The dilemma faced by policy makers

Because of the massive injections of money, the inflation genie may pop up, presenting policy makers with a complex dilemma - whether to continue to print money to support the economy and financial markets, or to stop or considerably reduce the printing of money in order to control the inflation.

## Possibility 1

Policy makers choose to continue to support the markets and continue to print money despite the pressures of inflation.

Under these conditions, the economy may face stagflation - a combination of recession and hyperinflation.

Even if we assume that the Stock Market won't collapse (because of the money injections), the hyperinflation will completely erode the value of the investments in the Stock Market. Thus, the hyperinflation will reconcile the gap between the prices of shares in the Stock Market and the state of the real economy.

There is also the possibility that the Stock Market will react to the stagflation with negative sentiment, causing the collapse of the prices in the equity market. After the collapse of the stocks, their prices will reflect the gloomy state of the real economy.

## Possibility 2

Due to the fear of inflation, policy makers choose to stop or considerably reduce the printing of money - with a very high price tag: the recession will be more severe, and the Stock Market will collapse.

In this possibility, the low stock prices represent the poor state of the real economy and the gap will be reconciled.

In the doomsday scenario, when mega inflation and deep recession take control of the economy, the Stock Market will become a less attractive alternative. Not only that - the market can collapse, making even the Safety Net assumption less relevant. Here too, the gap between the stock prices and the state of the economy will be reconciled.

## The NEW economic matrix serves three important goals:

The **first goal** of using the new economic matrix is to see a mapped outline of future scenarios and their probability.

The **second goal** of using the economic matrix is to understand the impact of the decisions made by policy makers, in the context of printing money.

The **third goal** of using the economic matrix is to understand the timeframe (or window of opportunities) that we have, as investors, to use our money to profit from the tremendous injections of money made by policy makers.

The first two economic scenarios support the three assumptions of the NEW Stock Market and provide us with the ideal conditions to implement the short-term profit investment strategy. The third scenario does not support the existence of the three conditions.

## Why long-term investment can lead us to poor decisions?

Based on the economic matrix, let's suppose we invest in stocks for the long run

### The optimistic scenario:

If the optimistic scenario (which is less likely in the short run) materializes and the economy will completely recover, then the high prices of the stocks (**before** the quick recovery) will already represent the optimistic scenario.

There will be no more justification for a long-term rally in the Stock Market, because Stock Market prices were high **prior to** the rapid economic recovery.

In other words, the high prices of the stocks in the optimistic scenario **already** represent the optimistic scenario as well as the assumption of money injections. Therefore, if there actually is a quick economic recovery, then, while it will probably impact the Stock

Market in a positive way, we probably won't see a long-lasting, significant rally because the prices of stocks were already high before the economic recovery.

## Conclusion

Even if the optimistic economic scenario materializes, we probably won't enjoy a long-term rally.

### The doomsday scenario:
#### *The very likely scenario after four to five years*

If, during the U-shaped economic recovery, additional and unexpected internal or external forces negatively impact the economy, then the injections of money will continue for a longer period of time (because the economy won't be able to stand on its own), making the probability of high inflation more likely.

The pressures of inflation will present policy makers with the dilemma whether to continue to support the economy and the financial markets or to stop the injections of money.

If they choose to stop the injections of money then the Stock Market will collapse and the recession will deepen.

No matter what choice the policy makers make,

we, as investors, will move to the doomsday scenario of deep recession or stagflation - from a U-shaped economic recovery to an L-shaped deep economic recession accompanied by hyperinflation.

If we invest our money in long-term stocks and the doomsday scenario of deep recession or stagflation materializes, as a result of either one of these scenarios, we will lose most of the money we invested in the Stock Market.

## Stagflation

A combination of hyperinflation and a deep recession.

## The realistic scenario:

### The most likely scenario in the medium run

If the most likely scenario - the realistic scenario - materializes and the injections of money continue for at least four to five years, we can take advantage and profit from the massive injections of money. **This book concentrates on this period of time.**

As we described earlier, if the economy doesn't recover within four to five years, we will probably fall into the doomsday scenario in which hyperinflation can erase all our profits.

Even worse, there is also the possibility that in order to counteract the hyperinflation, policy-makers will start to print less money: in this scenario stock prices will fall, and again, we will lose most of our money.

Another bad possibility the worst one of all - is that we will face stagflation, a combination of hyperinflation and a recession.

No matter the economic outcome, long-term investments place us at higher risk to lose money than profit from the short-term strategy.

**BE AWARE!**
*If we invest most of our money in a long-term investment at the expense of short-term profits, we won't be able to enjoy the possibility of taking advantage of, and profiting from, the cyclical fluctuations in the Stock Market.*

But if we take advantage of short-term opportunities (in the intermediate time range of four to five years) in the NEW Stock Market, then we can profit from policy-maker decisions to support the economy and the financial markets, while at the same time, shielding our money from the long-term **built-in risks** that exist in the NEW Stock Market and can pop up unexpectedly at any given time.

Long-term investments place us at higher risk to lose money than practicing the short-term strategy.

## What's next?

In Chapter 5 you will be introduced to the entities that control the NEW Stock Market.

# Conclusions concerning your investment decisions

## *IN: NEW Stock Market*

### The Policy makers control the market

A Stock Market that is supported by trillions of dollars injected into the economy and the financial markets and totally controlled by policy makers. Policy makers decisions and the injections of money create a kind of a Safety Net in the Stock Market.

### Short-term profits

The massive injections of money and the fluctuations in the prices of shares in the NEW Stock Market create opportunities for investors to enjoy short-term profits.

### The NEW economic matrix

The first two scenarios in the economic matrix support the existence of the three conditions. The third scenario - the doomsday scenario - doesn't support the three conditions.

## *OUT: OLD Stock Market*

### The real economic fundamentals are in good shape

The interventions by policy-makers are minimal. In most cases, the prices of shares reflect the conditions in the real economy.

### Long-term investments

We, or our financial advisors, buy stocks that are considered to be good investments in the long run. After holding the stocks for several years, we sell them and can enjoy a nice profit.

# Chapter 5

## Policy Makers - IN
## Free Markets - OUT

The NEW Stock Market is completely controlled by policy makers: it is supported by trillions of dollars injected into the economy and the financial markets.

## Who are the policy makers?

### The US Treasury

The US Treasury directly represents the agenda of the politicians. The Treasury is responsible for the decisions that impact the real economy - such as the transfer of trillions of dollars to individuals, households and businesses that lost their income due to the disastrous effects of the Covid-19 pandemic.

## The Federal Reserve

The Federal Reserve is the central banking system of the United States of America. The main mission of the central bank is to control the monetary system to alleviate or resolve financial crises. Put simply, when policy makers at the central bank inject trillions of dollars into the financial markets, there is a direct positive impact on the prices of securities. You, as an investor in the Stock Market, will see it expressed in positive sentiment in the Stock Market.

# What are the main goals of the policy makers?

### In the real economy:

Low unemployment, a growing GDP, low inflation, preservation of the good standing of the US dollar in the world, profitable companies.

### In the financial markets:

Policy makers contribute to the stability of prices in the bond market and in the Stock Market to prevent their collapse. Preventing the collapse of these very important financial markets protects pension funds.

Policy makers allocate resources to maintain high

liquidity of valuable money for firms that, in financial crisis, want to raise money.

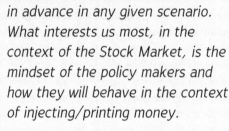

**IN MY EXPERIENCE**
*When we know the goals of the policy makers, it gives us the ability to predict their actions in advance in any given scenario. What interests us most, in the context of the Stock Market, is the mindset of the policy makers and how they will behave in the context of injecting/printing money.*

If, for example, the growth of the economy improves to a greater degree than expected, it is reasonable to assume that the policy makers will tend to print less money to support the economy. However, if, for example, unemployment rates rise considerably, they will continue to print and inject more money into the real economy.

It is important to note that we never know the specific time at which the intervention will happen and we also don't know what the scale of the support will be. One of the reasons for this uncertainty is that policy makers can also act based on political interests. If there are going to be elections for example, policy makers can behave in a more generous manner, and vice versa.

**BE AWARE!**
As investors in the NEW Stock Market, we have to monitor the situation to determine when the policy makers will decide to STOP supporting the financial markets and the economy.

## Why would policy makers stop printing money?

When the genie of inflation appears, or currency troubles start to pop up, policy makers will have to choose between two options: whether to keep injecting money - or to stop.

**What will happen to the financial markets if policy makers decide to stop or considerably reduce the injections of money?**

If this happens **before** the economy fully recovers, we may face a very sharp fall in the financial markets alongside devasting effects on the economy.

## OLD and NEW weapons used by policy makers

As previously noted, what mostly symbolizes the new economic and financial reality of our days is the decision of policy makers worldwide, and particularly in the US, to inject trillions of dollars into the economy and the financial markets.

The money printing solution, in the meantime, prevents the real economy from deteriorating further and gives the investors in the NEW Stock Market a Safety Net.

However, all these positive results come with a price tag. The large injections of money have the ability to awake an old and a very powerful enemy of the economy and the Stock Market - the genie of inflation.

Before the injections of trillions of dollars, the main weapon used by policy makers to cope with or avoid economic and financial crises was that of interest rates - a powerful and effective weapon.

## The difference between the OLD and the NEW financial reality

In the days of the old Stock Market, investors took note of announcements made by policy makers (as they should also do in the new reality) as well as economic indicators, such as the GDP - economic growth, the rate of unemployment, the firm's profitability and other relevant indicators. Based on this data, they would try to figure out if the central bank would likely raise, lower, or not change the interest rate. The prediction impacted the activity and direction of the general financial markets.

In the new reality, the question to ask is different: Will the policy makers continue to print money (to support the economy and the market), and at what levels?

## The Good Times - from the 1980s to 2020

Over the course of these 40 years, the most powerful and effective weapon used to prevent inflation was that of interest rates. Most of the time, peace and tranquility ruled the economic kingdom.

During this period - which ended not so long ago - policy makers at the Fed (central bank) responded to economic challenges with a powerful and simple tool - changing the interest rates.

If the economy was showing signs of overheating that could lead to inflation pressures, then the Fed would immediately raise the interest rates; after a relatively short time, the economy would return to a healthy course. If, on the other hand, the economy was showing signs of moving to an economic slowdown that could lead to an economic recession, the solution was also very simple - the Fed would lower the interest rates. Here too effects were seen within a short period of time.

Of course, here and there more severe measures were employed to cope with financial discrepancies/disasters, such as the 2008 mortgage crisis. But in the end, even in 2008 the economic recovery was a very rapid "V-shaped" recovery. Accordingly, the financial markets also reacted with a corresponding rapid "V-shaped" recovery - and peace and tranquility returned to the economic kingdom and financial markets.

## The new, challenging reality

Today, the main tool used in the past - changing interest rates - has become obsolete in fighting recession, because over the years interest rates have come close to zero and, in some countries, are even negative. Therefore, in order to deal with the main economic challenges created by Covid-19 and resolve the impending economic crisis, policy makers must turn to other, less effective tools.

71

## The new weapons at the disposal of policy makers in the new reality

As described above, the traditional powerful and effective weapon used to fight economic crises - interest rates - is obsolete in today's reality. These have been replaced with two other weapons that are less effective, and that if used unwisely, ultimately result in significant inflation, doing more harm than good.

## The two chosen weapons in the new reality:

Monetary easing - The central bank injects trillions of dollars to buy bonds in the financial markets, with a main impact on equity markets. When this weapon is used, we expect that the financial markets will respond positively.

In the context of our investments, the most important thing that this kind of policy creates is a positive sentiment in the Stock Market, which also elevates stocks prices. In a sense, printing money creates a Safety Net, if we assume that the injections of money will continue.

# There are two main impacts of monetary easing on your investments in the Stock Market and bond market:

## *Prices in the equity markets can go up considerably*

The impacts of a very accommodative (generous) monetary policy can create a surrealistic reality that masks the bad shape of the real economy (high unemployment, shrinking GDP, firms losing money); the prices of equity markets may do so well that they even break historical records. This gap between the real economy and the prices in the equity market should, in the end, be reconciled.

## *The yields in bonds (both government and corporate) will be flattened*

The main impact on your investment portfolio - due to the low yields on bonds, you, as an investor, know in advance that holding bonds in your investment portfolio will represent low returns in the future. At the same time, monetary easing has a positive effect - it reduces the volatility of the bonds. The practical meaning for you as an investor is that as long as the monetary easing is in place, if you hold bonds (government or corporate) the risk/volatility will be less, but your returns will be low.

## Fiscal policy

Mainly impacts the real economy. The government uses the Treasury to give households and business owners much-needed money to compensate for loss of income. These very justified money injections give households and business owners the ability to survive financially, as well as the important ability to spend more money by buying goods and using services. This latter effect is what helps boost the real economy.

## Fiscal policy in the context of your money investment

Fiscal policy can give a much-needed boost to the economy, but at the same time, using this tool over time can also create inflationary pressures. So, our money investment (portfolio), as we explain in more detail later, should be planned ahead of time to include financial products that protect us from this possibility.

## The creation of the NEW Stock Market and its implications

The bottom line of those two policies - the monetary easing policy and the fiscal policy - is that the policy makers act to save both, the economy and the financial markets. To achieve noticeable results, in the end they have no choice but to resort to a policy that mainly involves printing massive amounts of money. The Safety Net condition in the NEW Stock Market was created as a result of the massive injections of money.

A Safety Net - If things get worse, then the policy makers will intervene. This means that practically speaking, there is a virtual limit to how low stock prices can drop.

The interest rates on treasury notes and yields on bonds are near zero and even negative. The consequence is that investors in the financial markets who want to make meaningful profits, are in a sense forced to invest in stocks, because the other alternatives aren't attractive enough.

The prices of stocks don't only represent the true value of the firm's future profitability: they also represent the Safety Net assumption - according to which if something bad happens, policy makers will intervene.

The implication is that even if there is positive news and as a result, a rally of prices in the Stock Market or a specific sector, this rally will reach its peak sooner rather than later because the prices of stocks are high to begin with.

## Warning!

The securities and investment strategies mentioned in this book do not constitute suggestions or any type of recommendation regarding what you should or should not invest in.

If you are not an experienced investor, it is highly recommended that you build and accompany your investment decisions with the help and guidance of a licensed financial advisor.

# How the new reality can impact your investments

## Monetary policy

Corporate and government bonds usually represent an important component of the solid part of an investment portfolio. Due to the policy of monetary easing, their future returns are lower, but at the same time, their volatility is reduced. Put in other words - the bonds become less risky but less profitable as well.

Even investing in stocks is riskier than other alternatives. In the NEW Stock Market, stocks become the only alternative in which a meaningful profit can be made, compared to other alternatives.

## Fiscal policy

Under certain conditions (which will be discussed later), one of the side effects of the fiscal policy - the injection of trillions of dollars into the real economy in order to activate the cog-wheels of the economy - can create the possibility of future inflation. If we have a reason to expect inflationary pressures and that inflation is on the horizon, then we can also put IL bonds (inflation-linked corporate and government bonds) in our investment portfolio. Other options include anti-inflationary commodities, such as gold and crude oil. We can hold them in our investment portfolio and use them as an insurance policy against future inflation.

# What's next?

Chapter 6 will explain why using ETFs is the best way to benefit from the injections of money made by policy makers.

## Conclusions concerning your investment decisions

### *IN: NEW Stock Market*

**Printing money**

The monetary easing used by the Federal Reserve (central bank) in the financial markets, and fiscal policy is implemented by the US Treasury in the real economy.

**Policy makers**

Intervention in the economy and in the markets. The main policy involves the injection of trillions of dollars to the economy and to financial markets. This creates a NEW Stock Market, with a new financial matrix.

### *OUT: OLD Stock Market*

**Lowering interest rates**

Used in the past to fight recession, this strategy has become less relevant.

**Free economic forces**

The prices in the Stock Market reflect the economy and the profitability of firms.

# Chapter 6

## Investing in sectors - IN
## Picking stocks - OUT

In the new financial and economic reality, the most powerful tool at the disposal of policy makers is the injection (when needed) of large amounts of money into the economy and the financial markets. The investors in the Stock Market consider these injections of money (or their possibility) a kind of a Safety Net.

The investors know in advance that policy makers will use their tremendous power to support the Stock Market if something bad happens to the economy or the financial markets.

*IN MY EXPERIENCE*
*Understanding the mindset of policy makers gives you, as an investor, the ability to know what moves the markets, why, and in which direction.*

## Why, when buying stocks for the short term, should you focus on sectors and not on picking specific stocks?

There are three main reasons why short-term investments (for less than one year) should be made in sectors (using ETFs) and not in specific stocks.

## Maximize your profits using ETFs on indexes or sectors

### Reason 1

Policy maker actions don't support specific stocks: they support the macro behavior of the economy and the financial markets. It should be assumed that the actions taken by policy makers will positively impact the entire Stock Market.

If you buy a specific security in the Stock Market, then even if the Stock Market displays an overall rise (because the policy makers injected additional money), the price of your specific stock could remain the same or even go down.

Therefore, if you want to increase your chances of profiting, the solution is to invest in a general index (like the S&P) or in sectors (such as banks or automobile), and not in specific stocks.

## Reason 2

When you buy stocks to hold for the long run, you can use a more aggressive strategy than when you invest for the short term (less than one year).

An investor who plans on holding a particular security for several years has time to recover any loss in value, which can often happen with aggressive or risky investments. But when you invest in the short term you need a less risky investment. Buying and holding ETFs on an index or a sector gives you this preferred, less risky investment.

## Reason 3

Economic indicators (consumer confidence, GDP, the rate of unemployment, inflation, other economic events) impact different sectors in the Stock Market in different ways.

Sectors that can be impacted include, for example - technology, banking, consumption, airline companies, etc. Buying and selling ETFs on sectors enables us, as investors, to exploit those macroeconomic events to our benefit and make short-term profits. More than that, it gives us the ability to create alpha returns, which are higher than the general Stock Market returns.

The most important question that should lead your

investment decisions in the NEW Stock Market is not the question of which individual stocks to pick and buy, but what investment indexes/sectors are the best ones to invest in.

**IN MY EXPERIENCE**
*If you want to create short term profits ,investing your money in indexes and sectors using ETFs is a better strategy than investing in individual stocks.*

## Using ETFs to implement sector-based investment strategies

Sector-based investments using ETFs can help you, as an investor in the NEW Stock Market, accomplish two important Goals:

**To buy** ETFs in sectors whose stock prices have been going down considerably. These sectors will probably be impacted positively in the foreseeable future as a result of the policy makers' decisions.

**To sell** the ETFs (which we bought when their prices were low) after a considerable rise in prices.

# Maximize your profits: pursue alpha

## Alpha

The excess return on an investment relative to the return on a benchmark index.

For example, if you invest in a specific sector, and it returns 15 percent while the S&P 500 earned five percent, then the alpha will be 10 percent.

## Pursue alpha:

Picking the right sectors at the right time creates opportunities. One simple strategy is to hold the S&P index - in this situation, we move with the overall market. A second option is to deliver alpha by overweighting winning sectors and underweighting losers.

If we believe there is a sector or a major index for which it is the right time and price to start buying in the NEW Stock Market - for example, the technological sector - then we can act by using an ETF that closely represents the sector - such as the Nasdaq index.

**BE AWARE!**
*Using an ETF enables us to harness diversification benefits and take advantage of thematic trends without being too exposed to stock-specific risks.*

# Why it's less risky to invest in ETFs

## The risk of a stock

Every stock risk can be divided into two parts:

## The market risk

A fall in the market due to macroeconomic events. For example, if the growth of the economy is less than expected, this can have a negative impact on the Stock Market in general.

## The specific risk

The risk attributed to the company whose stock you are holding. For example, the company has a bad financial quarter. When, for example, you hold an ETF that contains over 50 bank stocks, if bank sector prices rise because of positive sentiment from an act by policy makers or good data about the real economy, you, as an investor, will profit from it.

But on the other hand, if you buy a specific stock, in the bank sector for example, it might go down while the entire sector goes up.

You may be ready to take this risk because you believe you can find stocks that are undervalued - which in the long run can perform better than the other bank stocks. In a normal Stock Market this approach would be quite reasonable. But in the new reality, the injections of money create a situation in which it is unlikely that you will be able to find undervalued stocks. Moreover, there could be inflation, or the Stock Market can collapse. Therefore, it is less likely that the use of this investment strategy will be successful.

**BE AWARE!**
*Your chances to profit from the money injections are greater when you use an ETF to invest in a certain sector, since it also gives you great diversification, which reduces your risk compared to holding individual stocks.*

## Final conclusions regarding the use of ETFs

Picking stocks is not an easy job. You may get the sector call right, but the stock call wrong.

ETFs can be used for precise implementation of sector-based investment strategies. Using ETFs to invest in sectors can help you, as an investor in the NEW Stock Market, achieve the desired exposure to risk without exposure to stock-specific risk.

For example, rather than selecting three or four companies from the technological sector, you can focus on the entire sector and buy an ETF on the Nasdaq in order to capture a positive trend in the technology sector. This kind of approach seeks to provide targeted exposure to a sector, while minimizing your exposure to stock-specific risk.

## What's next?

In chapter 7 you will learn how you can take advantage of the cyclical trends in the NEW Stock Market.

## Conclusions concerning your investment decisions

### *IN: NEW Stock Market*

**Overweighting winning sectors**

Deliver alpha (an excess return over the S&P) by overweighting winning sectors and underweighting losers.

**Minimizing risk**

Using ETFs to buy stocks in order to diversify.

Taking advantage of the injections of money

Use of ETFs to benefit from the injections of money made by policy makers.

### *OUT: OLD Stock Market*

**Picking long-term stocks**

The economic matrix shows us that there are inherent dangers in long-term investments.

# Chapter 7

## Cyclical Trends - IN
## Secular Trends - OUT

In the NEW Stock Market, the most useful distinction for investors will be the distinction between cyclical and non-cyclical sectors.

For example, suppose Stock Market investors think that the real economy will recover quickly because the Covid-19 vaccine is very effective. In that case, stocks in cyclical sectors such as banks or cars will benefit from a positive sentiment.

## Cyclical vs. non-cyclical stocks

The terms cyclical and non-cyclical refer to how closely a company's share price is tied to the changes and fluctuations of the economy. Cyclical companies are affected by broad economic changes that do not affect non-cyclical companies.

## Cyclical stocks

Cyclical stocks and their companies are affected by the economy. When the economy shows positive signs, the price of cyclical stocks will go up. An economic downturn will have a negative effect on their stock prices.

Companies of cyclical stocks sell goods and services that the general public buys when the economy is doing well, but reduces or stops purchasing when there is an economic downturn.

For example, airlines, restaurants, hotel chains, and cars are goods and services that people consume less when economic growth slows down. As a result of this drop in spending, the revenues of companies that produce and sell these goods and services fall. This puts negative pressure on their stock prices.

## Non-cyclical stocks

Non-cyclical stocks are profitable regardless of economic trends because they produce or distribute **basic** goods and services that consumers always require. Examples of basic goods are things such as food, electric power, water, and gas.

Stocks of utility companies are a great example. People need power and heat for themselves and their families, so even when economic growth slows, non-cyclical stocks can outperform cyclical stocks.

## Secular and cyclical trends

A secular trend is a long-term trend that indicates a particular sector of the economy is changing. A prominent example of a secular change was the disappearance of the horse-and-buggy with the advent of the automobile industry. A cyclical trend occurs rapidly. Therefore, the terms secular and cyclical trends can refer to long-term or short-term trends in the economy and in the Stock Market, respectively.

A secular change is a company's long-term direction of development in a specific industry, whereas a cyclical trend is a short-term direction of the stock prices in a specific industry. We can predict that, in the long run, the technology industry will be in a secular upswing. By contrast, the stocks of this industry in the short-term have cyclical ups and downs.

In the NEW Stock Market, we prefer to profit from cyclical short-term trends where the prices of shares frequently fluctuate. We don't want to base our investment decisions on secular long-term trends.

**BE AWARE!**
*It's important not to confuse cyclical trends with cyclical stocks. Cyclical trends refer to the dimension of time - the short-term. Cyclical or non-cyclical stocks refers to the correlation between stocks and the economy.*

## The positive sentiment in the market

In the financial markets, the yields on bonds are near zero and sometimes may even be negative. So, when there is a sale in the Stock Market, the money pulled from the Stock Market by investors doesn't have many other financial investment alternatives. This means that it's only a matter of time until most of the money pulled from the Stock Market will be reinvested in the market again.

Pension funds and big investment banks hold a lot of money, and have few alternative places to invest. To create profits for their customers, they **will be forced** to invest their money in the Stock Market.

At the same time, we have the Safety Net assumption-that policymakers, if needed, will support the economy and the Stock Market. The combination

91

of the lack of investment alternatives in the financial markets and the potential future injection of money by policymakers will create a positive sentiment in the Stock Market.

In such a Stock Market, the important question is: Which sectors should we focus on in the pursuit of alpha returns?

The answer is straightforward: The sector or sectors whose prices decreased considerably.

The Safety Net assumption (because of the policymakers' injections of money) doesn't mean that the Stock Market won't go down considerably. The fact that the policymakers are directly and indirectly involved in the financial markets minimizes the chances of a total Stock Market collapse, even if bad things occur in the economy.

## When is the right time to buy, or what is the right price to purchase at?

Let's suppose the technological sector enjoys a positive sentiment. The prices of the technology stocks rise considerably. Is that the right time to buy?

In a normal economy and a normal Stock Market, you look at the long-term secular trend. Suppose you predict that the technology sector will do well in the long run. This means you pay less attention to the prices you buy the technological stocks at today because you will hold them for years ahead.

But if your investment strategy is short-term profits, the price you buy the stocks at can be considered a crucial element.

## Why?

Because of the money injections, the stock prices are **already** being traded at high levels. So, even a positive sentiment in the technological sector (that can result from good economic news or greater than expected profitability of firms in the industry) will exhaust itself sooner than later.

If, for example, we buy shares in the technology sector after their prices rise considerably, then our chance of making a profit in the short-term is slim.

But if we assume the Safety Net and the lack of attractive alternative conditions exist, then we could use the fluctuations in the NEW Stock Market to our advantage.

If we encounter a sector that has a cyclical short-term negative trend and it went down considerably (five percent or more), we can buy its stocks using ETFs.

**IN MY EXPERIENCE**

*Most of the time, it is preferred to buy ETFs after a down correction and not after a rally when the prices are at their peak.*

Based on the two conditions outlined above, we can predict that the sector in the foreseeable future will enjoy a positive sentiment. We know it's only a matter of weeks or months before the positive sentiment is expected to return to this sector again. And then it will be the right time for us to materialize our profits.

**IN MY EXPERIENCE**

*There are hedge funds that use the rule of five percent. They can pick stocks or commodities*

*they desire to buy after they go down by at least five percent, and sell stocks or commodities after they rise by five percent or more. It is your call/decision in what intervals you want to buy and sell the securities in the Stock Market.*

**BE AWARE!**
*Five percent can also be an accumulation of several days. For example, the total decline in the Nasdaq is 5 percent after one week.*

# The decision-making process

To increase the chances of enjoying the positive effects of the policymakers' support in the Stock Markets, it's recommended to use ETFs.

You can adopt a strategy that says I will wait until bad news negatively impacts the sector you want to purchase in. Then you can, for example, buy the stocks after they plunge by five percent or more.

The underlying logic is that in the near future of days, weeks, or a few months (from the day you bought the stocks), something good will happen, and these stocks will rise again.

When we decide practically to buy an ETF, we can control the timing of when to do so.

In the Stock Market, which is supported by the most powerful economic forces in the world (the FED and US Treasury) through injections of trillions of dollars, the prices of stocks are mostly at their peak level or near to it. So, when prices rise over their peak to another peak, then it is highly likely that a correction will come after a while.

If you pick stocks after a considerable down correction, you win twice. You prevent the losses of a possible correction and buy at a more reasonable price - a price that will, in the short-term, give you the possibility to profit from holding them.

With sector-based investment strategies, you as an investor can adjust your portfolio according to shifts in economic conditions by increasing allocations to cyclical sectors favored by the positive economic data and reducing allocations to sectors facing macro headwinds.

## What's next?

Chapter 8 explains why the world's economy is heading in a bad direction of less cooperation among countries, less growth, and an increased tendency towards inflation pressures.

## Conclusions concerning your investment decisions

### *IN: NEW Stock Market*

#### Cyclical trends

If we want to take advantage of policymakers' money injections, we must concentrate on short-term cyclical sector trends. The preferred time to buy is when the trend of the stock prices of a sector goes down. We assume that in the foreseeable future, something good will happen. We don't know precisely why or when it will happen. However, when it happens, we will sell our stocks and enjoy a profit.

### *OUT: OLD Stock Market*

#### Secular trends

Because of the money injections, we can face inflation or, even worse, stagflation (high inflation + recession). Investing in long-term stocks can turn out to be a poor decision.

# Chapter 8

## Deglobalization - IN
## Globalization - OUT

If we look at the world economic environment for the last four decades, starting from the 1980s, we'll notice that one of the most important economic indicators is the low inflation rates. The main force responsible for this was globalization. With globalization came reduced costs and increased growth all over the world.

During those four decades, we experienced globalization of the workforce, technological innovation, commercial treaties, and other such developments. The end result of all these was improved growth and reduced inflation pressures. In short, we've been living in an anti-inflationary global environment.

However, this positive, anti-inflationary trend has changed in the last few years as the global economy has become less united and more fragmented. In other words, we're heading back toward deglobalization.

# Reasons for Deglobalization

## 1. Effectiveness of political institutions has been weakened

Political institutions that are supposed to deal with globalization at either a national or an international level don't function as they should. For example, the effectiveness of the G20 (the premier forum for international economic and financial cooperation around the world). has been weakened mainly due to new institutions with a similar agenda that have appeared, but with no clear roadmap for cooperation between the different entities. This has had a great impact on trade protection, the regulation of capital flows, restrictions on information access, and the limitations of people's movements between countries.

Moreover, the WTO's **(World Trade Organization)** effectiveness has been diminished by the adoption of unilateral trade measures in some countries. For example, global efforts to tackle climate change have been compromised by the US's decision to abandon the UN Paris Agreement on Climate Change.

## 2. Protectionist policies

Globalization and trade integration have contributed to the increase in income inequality through skill-based and geographical distributional impacts. This rising inequality with increasing unemployment has created discontent and opposition to trade and globalization. The implications of these developments have led government policymakers around the world to support policies such as protectionism.

## 3. Rivalry between the US and China

In the past, global economic growth has been broad-based and synchronized across the world. However, much has changed in recent years. Trade tensions between the US and China have escalated, which has prompted the US's decision to impose import tariffs on steel and aluminum. These and other developments have greatly increased the possibility of a slowdown in global growth.

## 4. Lack of international cooperation and implementation

Demographics, migration, and climate change are examples of issues that have to be attended to with full cooperation between countries. These matters cannot be dealt with by individual countries working in isolation. Even the basic implementation of clear and fair trade laws, taxation, and foreign investments have not been consistently applied. The lack of cooperation between countries has directly impacted citizens in terms of employment and widening inequalities, and has caused citizens around the world to become anti-globalization.

## Global Trade Imbalances that Increase Trade Tensions between Countries

A trade deficit happens when a country is importing more goods and services than it is exporting. When countries run large deficits, businesses, trade unions, and politicians often point fingers at trading partners, accusing them of unfair practices. This can lead to tensions between countries and as a result, less economic cooperation.

For example: the tension between the United States and China, with regard to which country is primarily responsible for their trade imbalance, demonstrates the broader consequences for the international financial system when some countries run large account deficits and others accumulate big surpluses. The excessive global imbalances between countries can result in a threat to global economic stability.

## How Does Deglobalization Impact Our Investments?

Healthy globalization increases growth and reduces inflation pressures. When we look at the future, however, we can see that there are forces in the global economy that are decreasing globalization, consequently moving the world economy closer to deglobalization and more inflation pressures.

The positive, anti-inflationary trend has changed in the last few years as the global economy has become more fragmented.

## What's Next?

In Chapter 9, we'll discuss what might ensue if the dollar's global status as a leading reserve currency is compromised.

## Conclusions concerning your investment decisions

### *IN: NEW Stock Market*

Deglobalization

A world economic environment with less cooperation between countries, decreased growth, and an increase in inflation pressures.

### *OUT: OLD Stock Market*

Globalization

A global economic environment with high cooperation between countries, increased growth, and a reduction in inflation pressures.

# Chapter 9

## The genie of inflation - IN
## Dollar as a safe haven - OUT

Very few countries in the world can practice an economic policy that involves injections of trillions of dollars into their financial markets and real economy. Most other countries that try to engage in such practices on the same scale as the US will probably quickly face currency problems and mega inflation.

## The special status of the US dollar

The reason that the policy makers in the US can afford to inject trillions of dollars into the economy and the financial markets is because of the special status that the US dollar has in the world.

Most countries that try to do the same will very soon face negative consequences of currency instability, and possibly hyperinflation.

The special status of the US dollar as a reserve currency in the world enables policy makers in the US to practice a policy of injecting very large sums of money without suffering the short-term consequences.

## What is a reserve currency status?

The US dollar enjoys the status of a **reserve currency.** A reserve currency (or an anchor currency) is a foreign currency that is held in significant quantities by central banks or other monetary authorities as part of their foreign exchange reserves.

The reserve currency can be used in international transactions and investments.

There is a huge demand for US dollars and for US government debt because countries around the world must keep huge reserves of US currency for the sake of international trade.

If, for example, in Greece, they want to buy cars from a US company, they need to pay with dollars. But even when they want to buy cars from South Korea for example, they can pay in dollars. If they try to pay with their local currency it probably would not be accepted.

Currently, foreign banks, situated outside the US, hold most of their assets in US currency. According to the International Monetary Fund (IMF), more than 60 percent of all foreign bank reserves are in US dollars.

# The forces that threaten the status of the US dollar as the world's reserve currency

## External forces

The Chinese renminbi (RMB) or the euro can be considered alternatives to the US dollar. The euro is the second most important reserve currency after the US dollar, representing about 21 percent of international foreign currency reserves.

China is determined to promote their official currency - the RMB in the world, by changing the way that international trade is conducted.

They shift more of their foreign reserves from dollars into RMB as the RMB gains greater attraction in global trade.

As an example, China is Africa's biggest trading partner. Due to China's influence, several central banks in Africa use the RMB as part of their reserve currency.

The United Nations and the IMF are advocating for a New World Reserve Currency. The UN and IMF have been issuing reports that openly call for finding alternatives to the US dollar as the world's reserve currency and no longer rely on the US dollar as the single major reserve currency.

All these forces can be considered external forces

that threaten to diminish the reserve status of the US dollar.

## Internal Forces

Printing trillions of dollars to support the economy and financial markets over a long period might awaken the genie of inflation.

It is important to note that the core problem of a shrinking gross domestic product (GDP) because of the enforced Covid-19 lockdown **will not be solved** by the fiscal policy of printing money to add to the economy.

While the GDP is shrinking or slowing, injections of money into the economy allow people and businesses (whose assets were frozen by the enforced lockdowns) to preserve their buying power.

Here is the big problem - because the GDP is shrinking while consumers preserve their buying power, the same amount of money competes for fewer goods and services. So, it is clear that if these conditions continue, the prices of goods and services will rise and inflation pressures will appear.

## What are the implications?

If the status of the dollar as a reserve currency is compromised, it will have a great impact on the US economy.

The implications could be:

**1.** Massive inflation.

**2.** Higher interest rates on mortgages.

**3.** Increase in the cost of food, clothing and gasoline.

**4.** Higher interest rates on debts.

## How this impacts the policy makers' decisions

The federal reserve in the US is also aware of these possible negative implications. So, when policy makers think that the status of the dollar worldwide can be hurt, this can impact their decisions to be **more conservative** in terms of the sums of money injected into the economy and the financial markets.

For the US, the reserve status of the dollar can be rightly considered as a goose that lays golden eggs, therefore, policy makers will do anything to preserve it.

## What's Next?

Chapter 10 will explain why a "U-shape" (slow) economic recovery that led to high volatility of Stock Market prices will serve short-term investment strategies.

# Conclusions concerning your investment decisions

## IN: NEW Stock Market

### The genie of inflation

Injections of money into the economy do not resolve the problem of the shrinking GDP. Therefore, although consumers preserve (in most cases) their buying power, fewer products and services are available. This can lead to increases in the prices of goods and services and the genie of inflation may appear.

## OUT: OLD Stock Market

### The dollar as a safe haven

Because printing large amounts of money and the existence of other competing currencies around the world, the status of the US dollar as a reserve currency is in question. But US policy makers will use any means in their economic arsenal to preserve the US dollar's status as the leading reserve currency in the world.

# Chapter 10

## U-shaped recovery - IN
## V-shaped recovery - OUT

The accommodative (very generous) support of the policy makers involves injecting trillions of dollars into the economy and the financial markets. This is not expected to last forever. Therefore, what should interest us as investors, is how long will this last (short-term or long-term) and when will it stop. The answer to these questions can have a big impact on our investment decisions.

## V-shaped recovery

If we expect that the economic recovery will be quick, as with a V-shaped recovery, then the policy makers can afford to stop printing money to support the economy and the financial markets, very soon.

Why? Because they know the economy is in a healthy condition or heading in that direction, so it no longer needs the support of money injections.

In a V-shaped, quick economic recovery, the policy makers' accommodative support will cease.

**BE AWARE!**
*It is important to notice that even in a V-shaped recovery, the safety net assumption will continue because investors assume that if something bad happens in the economy or in the Stock Market then the policy makers will intervene.*

## U-shaped recovery

If the expectations (based on the economic data) are that it will take years for the economy to recover, as leading economists predict, then we will expect a U-shaped recovery. This means that the actual economic recovery will be slow. It will be reasonable to assume that the policy makers will continue with their current accommodative policy - the injections of money will continue for the foreseeable future.

Why is this assumption reasonable? Because when the economic recovery follows a U-shape, if the policy makers decide to stop printing money or reduce it considerably, the financial markets can drop very quickly and the economy can fall into a deep recession.

The policy makers are aware of these negative implications if they stop supporting the economy and the markets (before the economy fully recovers). It will be reasonable for us, as investors, to assume that the money printing policy will continue.

## The implications to the investors

If we reach the conclusion that there is a high probability that the economic recovery will be slow, as in a U-shaped recovery rather than a quick V-shaped recovery, then as investors, we can assume the money printing policy will be with us for a long time. Thus, decisions regarding our investments should take this assumption into account.

If we assume a U-shaped recovery, the Stock Market will experience greater fluctuations in prices than it would with a V-shaped recovery.

For a short-term investment strategy, a U-shaped recovery produces more opportunities to profit and take advantage of this volatility in the prices of stocks.

## Why will the economic recovery be U-shaped?

Today, two major aspects have changed, making the economic landscape different from that of the last four decades.

**The first aspect** is that over the last several years, firms have become very leveraged, which gives them an inherent inclination to spend less and save more. They accomplish this mainly by firing or reducing their labor force. If they need additional workers in the future, rather than hiring new full-time workers with full benefits, they will employ freelancers and part-time employees, etc. This in turn, creates an environment of households that also spend less and (try to) save more because they are not confident of their economic future.

**The second aspect** that differentiates this crisis from previous ones, is that in the last four decades, most crises were of a financial nature. Therefore, if a "hole" was created, then the challenges the policy makers faced was relatively simple: US policy makers used the central bank to "plug the hole."

The Federal Reserve stepped in and closed the hole by using monetary means. Simply put, the policy makers took full responsibility for the irresponsible actions of players in the financial markets, such as investment banks and other big financial institutions.

The Federal Reserve used tax payers' money to fix the problem.

In the new era, because of the enforced lockdowns and other limitations, this Covid-19 crisis has direct implications on the real economy in terms of less demand for goods and services. However, an effective solution is to give large grants. The second problem is a shrinking or a slowdown in the GDP, which is the type of problem that the policy makers cannot step in and fix, so it cannot be resolved in the short-run.

The end result of these two new elements or economic forces is that the recovery process will be much slower compared to earlier times.

The economy will probably be in a U-shape rather than a V-shape and will take years to recover.

## V-shaped economic recovery

The problem (hole) is mostly financial.
The policy makers step in and fill the "hole".

### After the hole/problem is reconciled:

- Consumer confidence and money spending grows.
- Unemployment rates are low.
- The GDP continues to grow at a good rate.
- Inflation is rebound at a reasonable rate of two percent to three percent to a year.

## U-shaped economic recovery

- The problem ("hole") is mostly in the real economy
- The policy makers step in to alleviate the problem

### After the policy makers intervene:

- Unemployment rates continue to be high.
- The GDP (national cake) can still shrink or grow slowly.
- Inflation pressures can appear due to financial support.

## L-shape - additional internal and external negative forces impact the economy after all the big guns have been used

The financial and real economy are in ruins and all the tools available to save it have been used. In this kind of a scenario, the economy will probably be in stagflation - a situation where we have a recession accompanied by hyperinflation.

## What's Next?

In chapter 11, you will learn about the three inherent risks to the economy and to the Stock Market, over the long-term.

# Conclusions concerning your investment decisions

## IN: NEW Stock Market

### "U-shaped" (slow economic) recovery

The meaning of a U-shaped economic recovery is that the recession in the real economy is not going to disappear soon. This implies that the policy makers will continue to print money for years to come. In relation to our investments, the Monetary policy, which provides super accommodative support of the Federal Reserve in the financial markets, will continue with the important ramifications of this policy on the prices of the equity markets. The high volatility of prices in the Stock Market will serve the short-time investment strategy.

## OUT: OLD Stock Market

### "V-shaped" (quick economic) recovery

If we believe that the economic recovery is going to be a V-shape, we must assume that the injection of money into the economy and the financial markets is going to stop or decrease considerably. Thus, the volatility of the market will be reduced.

# Chapter 11

## Policy Makers' Dilemma - IN
## Low Inflation - OUT

The real rulers of the economy and the financial markets were always the policy makers. However, in the past their interventions were minimal and for the most part the public was not aware of them.

In the past, when policy makers identified the economy as healthy and moving in the right direction (low unemployment rates, a growing economy, low inflation) they did not intervene with the normal course of the economy or the financial markets.

The policy makers allowed the free forces of the economy and financial markets to follow their course.

If and when a problem arose, the policy makers intervened, but that frequently occurred inconspicuously.

Before the phenomenon of printing money, the financial markets were mostly a reflection of the real economy.

But in current times, in the new economic and financial reality into which trillions of dollars are injected, the policy makers' actions and intervention in the markets and in the economy are crucial.

The policy makers' decisions have a tremendous impact on the economy and the financial markets. As an investor in the NEW Stock Market, it is important for you to understand the policy makers' mindset and what impacts their decisions.

**BE AWARE!**
*Political concerns (rivalry between political parties) can also impact the policy makers' decisions, the timing of the injections and sometimes the sums of money that are injected.*

The political considerations add uncertainty to the market. But paradoxically, this can serve us as short-time investors because it increases fluctuations in the Stock Market. Therefore, we have more opportunities to benefit from the short-term investment strategy.

# The policy makers' future dilemma

Policy makers can continue to inject money until they hit the wall of inflation. First, they will probably try to delay approaching this wall of inflation by injecting money more conservatively. But when the policy makers see that the genie of inflation is nearing the horizon, they will face a dilemma.

If we assume that the economy will still be in recession and will still need injections of money, if the policy makers stop the money injections, the economy might deteriorate into a greater recession and the financial markets are likely to collapse.

On the other hand, if they continue injecting money, then the genie of inflation will probably appear, with the possibility that the status of the dollar as a reserve currency in the world could be compromised.

As investors, we should be aware of these possible risks, monitor them very closely and be prepared for them.

Our financial investments (portfolio) should contain suitable financial products. This will protect us from each of these possible outcomes.

If the money injections hit the wall of inflation while the economy is still weak (high unemployment rates and shrinking or slow GDP growth), the policy makers will face a dilemma:

119

# Here are their possible choices:

## Awaken the genie of inflation - first possible outcome

If the policy makers continue to inject money, then the genie of inflation will probably appear.

## Recession - second possible outcome

If the policy makers stop printing money (before the economy fully recovers) or reduce it considerably, the recession will become greater and the financial markets will probably collapse.

## Stagflation - third possible outcome

Additional external and internal forces will negatively impact the economy. As a result, the GDP will continue to be low and even shrink further.

**BE AWARE!**
The GDP represents all the commodities and services produced in a given period across the country. By definition, this economic cake is limited.

When the GDP - economic cake - continues to contract and becomes smaller, while the demand for goods and services remains the same, we have a situation where the prices of goods and services will rise.

In other words, the buying power of the dollar will be reduced and the end result will be inflation.

**IN MY EXPERIENCE**

*In normal times, in a healthy economy, the government will raise taxes or increase interest rates. These two mechanisms can prevent inflation pressures.*

However, when the economy is weak (high unemployment, shrinking GDP, low consumption), it is not likely that these very effective measures will be used.

The result is uncontrolled inflation in a shattered economy - this is the worst of both worlds and is called stagflation.

The chances that one of these three negative scenarios will materialize increases and becomes greater, if we assume that the economic crisis is going to last for a longer period.

## Why it is important to your investment portfolio

Printing money has a positive effect on the financial markets. At the same time, using the strategy of money injections **for a long period** can create the possibility of large inflation or recession or the worst of both situations - stagflation.

These possible outcomes can have a great impact on the decisions of the policy makers. The main implication of these three possible outcomes is that our exposure to the financial markets should be limited.

If we assume that the real economy will not recover soon, then each of the outcomes mentioned can materialize and have serious effects on our investments.

Therefore, our money investment decisions should consider these possibilities.

If you invest money in the financial markets, you want your private investment portfolio to include financial products that will protect your money in every possible scenario.

We should hold more cash and cash equivalents in our investment portfolio. As time passes, and the economic crisis doesn't resolve, the likelihood that one of these three outcomes will materialize increases.

## What is driving (impact) the markets?

If the economic indicators are going in the wrong direction (higher unemployment, lower productivity, low consumer confidence) that implies that the economy is slowing down and the scenario of a slow economic recovery becomes more relevant.

In such a scenario, non-cyclical stocks that do not depend on the real economy (for example food and utilities) will have a more positive effect on their stock prices.

If there are positive signs that the economy is strengthening or the investors assume that the policy makers will inject additional money soon, then it will be more likely that cyclical stocks that depend on the real economy, like banks or the automotive sector, will have a stronger positive sentiment in its stock prices.

If the policy makers reduce, delay or stop printing money to support the markets before the economy reaches a healthy state, the prices of securities throughout the Stock Market can react negatively.

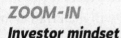

**ZOOM-IN**
*Investor mindset*
*The major investors in the Stock Market are aware of this matrix of possibilities. When they invest their money, they will take that matrix of possible economic scenarios into account.*

# Demonstration of the Matrix:

## The macroeconomic DATA

If, for example, the unemployment rate published in a certain month is significantly lower than expected, the impact - on the real economy - will be positive.

The cyclical stocks (those that are directly connected to the real economy) will benefit from positive developments in the real economy, for example, the automotive and banking sectors.

## WHY?

If more people work, then their ability to spend more increases, as well as their ability to repay commitments and buy new cars.

Therefore, it helps the real economy and businesses

and firms that are based on traditional consumer demands will probably earn more in the future because of the increased activity.

Thus, this news has a positive effect on the prices of stocks that are connected to the real economy, such as banks and car companies.

## Let us assume the opposite
### The current macroeconomic DATA

The rate of unemployment published in a certain month is significantly higher than expected.

### The Stock Market direction

The impact - on the real economy - will be negative. The type of stocks that will be negatively impacted from developments in the real economy are the cyclical stocks - for example the automotive and banking sectors.

## The impact on the policy makers

Here is a paradox because high unemployment indicates that the policy makers will begin to inject money sooner rather than later. The investors in the market do not know exactly when the policy makers will print additional money; therefore, the

125

initial, immediate impact on the Stock Market will probably be negative.

If the prices in the cyclical stock sectors decrease significantly (five percent or more), an investor might see it as an opportunity to buy stocks in these sectors at an attractive price and hold them until the trend changes and the positive sentiment on stock prices, returns to these sectors.

The positive change in shares' prices can occur because of a supportive move by the policy makers' positive future macro-economic data or an increase in a firm's profitability.

As investors, we do not know exactly what will trigger the change and when it will happen. But when it happens, we will sell and realize our profits.

## What's Next?

In chapter 12, you will get a review of the short-term investment strategy.

# Conclusions concerning your investment decisions

## *IN: NEW Stock Market*

### Short-term profits
Take advantage of the fluctuations in the NEW Stock Market by implementing the short-term investment strategy.

### High liquidity
Hold large amounts of cash and its equivalent to be prepared for any scenario.

## *OUT: OLD Stock Market*

### Long-term investments
In the long-run, there are three negative possibilities - inflation, recession, and stagflation.

# Chapter 12

## Buy low, sell high - IN
## Fundamental analysis - OUT

In this chapter we will review the short-term investment strategy.

In a reality in which policy makers are willing to inject massive sums of dollars into the economy and the financial markets, a Safety Net is created for the investors in the NEW Stock Market.

Investors know that the most powerful force in the economic world - US policy makers - the Treasury and the Federal Reserve - support both the economy and the financial markets.

**The short-term investment strategy applies if you assume the existence of three conditions.**

# The short-term strategy assumptions:

## Assumption no. 1

### The Safety Net condition

The assumption is that policy makers will continue printing money (if needed) to support the economy and the financial markets.

## Assumption no. 2

### A lack of attractive alternatives to the Stock Market

The assumption is that the interest rates and yields on bonds will be near zero and even negative. Therefore, the main source of profit in the financial markets will be the possibility and option to invest some of the money in the Stock Market.

## Assumption no. 3

### A quick rotation of positive sentiment between sectors

The assumption is that the positive sentiment in a sector lasts only for a short time - days or weeks.

If you assume that all three conditions will continue to exist, then the perfect environment is created to employ the strategy of short-term investments.

**BE AWARE!**

*The Safety Net condition doesn't guarantee that prices in the Stock Market won't fall, even considerably by five percent, 10 percent, or even more.*

## Warning!

The securities and investment strategies mentioned in this book do not constitute suggestions or any type of recommendation regarding what you should or should not invest in. It is highly recommended that if you are not an experienced investor you build and accompany your investment decisions with the help and guidance of a licensed financial advisor.

## When to buy ETFs on sectors

There are many different ways to decide when to buy stocks (technical, fundamental, macro-based), but when basing the decision on the existence of the three conditions, the best strategy is to buy stocks when sector prices go down considerably, by five percent, 10 percent or more.

The fall down in prices can happen in one day or

over several days. When it happens, we can begin buying ETFs in the affected sector(s).

## There are three ways in which the prices of shares in a sector can be negatively impacted:

In the first scenario, the prices of shares in the sector went up considerably, so there are investors who want to materialize their profits. However, new buyers are aware that the prices of the stocks in the specific sector are high: this creates negative sentiment, which causes the prices of the stocks in this sector to go down.

A second scenario is that there has been negative macro-economic news: while the entire Stock Market is affected, this sector is impacted more badly than others. A third possible scenario is that the profitability of firms in this sector is less than expected.

In practical terms, if one or even a combination of these scenarios may occur, an opportunity to buy shares at attractive prices can be created.

For you, as an investor, the green light to start buying ETFs on sectors, can be a considerable fall down in their share prices. The golden rule you can adopt for buying the ETFs can be a drop in shares prices of five percent - or more. it's your **money and your call.** Even then, you can divide the money you decided to invest in the sector and use only some of it to buy; later, if the stocks continue to fall down - let's say an additional five percent (10 percent all together) - you can buy more with the rest of the money set aside.

## When to sell ETFs on sectors

We can assume, with a high degree of likelihood, that it's only a matter of time before policy makers will intervene, and that other positive factors may also pop up - leading to a short rally of shares' prices` in the stocks of the sector you invested your money in, a rally that could be in the range of five percent to 10 percent or more. For you, this short rally will be the perfect time to sell your stocks and materialize your profits.

### THE GOLDEN RULE (THE SHORT-TERM PROFITS STRATEGY)

Buy stocks (using an ETF) when their prices drop considerably

Sell the stocks (the ETF) when their prices rise considerably

**BE AWARE!**
The decision to sell stocks when their prices rise considerably doesn't have to be made when the percent rise is equal to the percent the stocks had fallen when we decided to buy them. For example, if we bought an ETF on the Nasdaq after its stock prices dropped by five percent, we can decide to sell the ETF on the Nasdaq not when it rises by five percent, but only when it rises at least 10 percent.

## The positive sentiment in sectors

In normal times, the average duration of positive sentiment in a sector is three months. For example, a positive trend/sentiment for the technology sector displayed by investors in the Stock Market will result in a rise in the prices of stocks in the technology sector. However, in the end, this positive sentiment will exhaust itself, and the investors will move on to favor the bank sector, for example - until that too exhausts itself.

In the NEW Stock Market, the rotation of positive sentiment between sectors is considerably shorter, taking only weeks and, in some cases, even days.

## Why is the positive sentiment shorter in the NEW Stock Market?

The main reason for the short rotation time between sectors is that **from the beginning**, in the NEW Stock Market, the prices of stocks in all sectors are high (because of the injections of money). When the prices of the sector with the positive sentiment rise, they hit a ceiling of very high prices that makes them less attractive for investors - sooner rather than later. This causes investors to move to another sector, or sectors, that seem to have more attractive prices.

As an investor, you can use these dynamics of the NEW Stock Market to your advantage when making decisions regarding the buying and selling of stocks.

In a classical Stock Market that functions in a normal economy in which there are no money injections, the **investor anchor** (Safety Net) is the potential growth and profitability of the firms that stand behind the stocks or bonds that we, as investors, buy. Most of the time, the real economy and the financial markets move in the same direction.

In the NEW Stock Market, which is supported by and entirely dependent on policy makers` decisions, the rules of the game are different. The **investor anchor** is the assumption that policy makers will support the prices of the stocks and bonds in any given situation. The Stock Market is totally dependent on the policy makers' support.

Policy makers, whose decisions move the markets, are influenced mostly by the economic data. Therefore, if we assume that macroeconomic indicators impact policy makers` decisions on whether to inject money and how much, we know that if something bad happens in the economy or the financial markets, policy makers will intervene.

In this kind of economic and financial environment there can be a complete lack of correlation between the prices of the stocks and the real value of the firms that they represent.

### IN MY EXPERIENCE
*The intervention may take weeks or months, but in the end, when it happens, it will have a positive impact on the economy and eventually, on the Stock Market.*

135

# The paradoxical behavior of the NEW Stock Market

You, as an investor, don't know when policy makers will inject the money, or how much they will inject. The only thing that you can rely is that there is a high probability that it will happen in the foreseeable future.

## The paradox

If the macroeconomic data is worse than expected - for example, higher unemployment or more severe shrinking in GDP than predicted - it can be considered bad news for the Stock Market as well. So, it's reasonable to assume that the prices of stocks in the equity market will be impacted in a negative way.

**However,** at the same time, **<u>due to</u>** the economic data being so bad, we can reasonably assume that policy makers will act more aggressively to support the markets and inject more money - in the foreseeable future.

The opposite is also true: if the macroeconomic data is positive, it's reasonable to assume that the Stock Market will be positively impacted, while at the same time, the motivation of policy makers to inject additional money becomes less obvious.

This paradox creates a Stock Market with many ups and downs - and when you focus on short-term profits, a financial environment with a high rate of fluctuation can be the ideal environment for you.

# Take advantage of the paradox:
## Buy low, sell high

The practical way to meet the challenge posed by the paradox is to use it to your advantage. The solution for this financial reality is the short-term strategy called "buy low, sell high."

How low is "low"? A rule of thumb is to look for a considerable drop in price - more than five percent. You can never really know what the lowest price will be.

After purchasing stocks in a sector (preferably using an ETF), you wait for something positive to impact the sector share prices. You don't know when exactly the positive development will happen, but when positive sentiment returns to the stocks in the sector you purchased shares in, this will be the time to start consider selling the stocks and materialize your profit.

This kind of strategy, tailored to the conditions in the NEW Stock Market, gives you full control over how much money to invest in stocks (if at all), at what prices, and when to cash in.

## The sector rotation strategy

Investing by using sector ETFs can be an ideal way to execute a sector-based investment strategy. It gives us the ability to capture alpha opportunities, where we profit more than the general Stock Market.

**BE AWARE!**
*Using an ETF to buy stocks creates significant diversification that minimizes our exposure to specific risk.*

## Decisions: How, When, How Much

How much money to invest in the Stock Market and when depends on your personal risk tolerance, investment goals, and your investment time limit. It should be noted that over shorter periods, the performance of either cyclical stocks or non-cyclical stocks will also depend, in a large part, on the point in the cycle that the Stock Market happens to be in. For example, non-cyclical stocks tend to outperform during a "bear market" (prolonged price declines) and economic recessions; while cyclical stocks tend to excel during a "bull market" (a sustained increase in prices) or

138

during periods (or in the presence of signs) of economic expansion. This factor should, therefore, be taken into account by shorter-term investors or those seeking to time the markets.

## What's next?

In the next chapter I will describe the investment decisions that are appropriate for the 3 conditions. Understanding the investment decisions will give you the ability, as an investor, to take advantage of the NEW Stock Market and maximize your profits.

The third assumption gives us, as investors, the ability to produce alpha returns on our financial investment.

# Conclusions concerning your investment decisions

### IN: NEW Stock Market

**Short-term profit strategy**

Buy stocks (using an ETF) when their prices drop considerably

Sell the stocks (the ETF) when their prices rise considerably

### OUT :OLD Stock Market

Long-term investments.

# Chapter 13

## Short-Term Profits - IN
## Long-Term Profits - OUT

In today's NEW Stock Market, we witness a phenomenon that has never been seen before, in which the high prices of stocks do not reflect the unstable state of the real economy (plagued by unemployment, poor economic growth, businesses struggling to survive, and low consumer confidence).

In this unstable economy we even see some of the leading Stock Market indexes breaking historical records.

The discrepancy between the high prices of Stock Market shares and the unstable condition of the real economy can be largely explained by the decision of policy makers to inject trillions of dollars into the financial markets and to the economy.

It seems that the uncertainty in the real economy is going to stay with us for the foreseeable future. As a result, the massive injections of money may stay with us for a prolonged period of time.

These massive injections of trillions of dollars have created a NEW Stock Market that is full of opportunities - and risks. The NEW Stock Market requires new investment strategies.

The long-standing main investment strategy according to which long-term investments in the Stock Market are the best way to invest money has become less relevant in the NEW Stock Market.

The effective investment strategy that answers the conditions in the NEW Stock Market is the short-term profit strategy.

In Chapters 1 and 2 we introduced the NEW Stock Market matrix and presented three conditions whose existence supports the strategy of short-term profits.

In this chapter we will explore the investment decisions that should follow, as long as the three conditions exist in the NEW Stock Market.

## The "Safety Net" impact on stock prices

The "Safety Net" condition assumes that if things in the economy or the financial markets worsen, then the policy makers (the Federal Reserve, US Treasury) will intervene.

The belief that policy makers will continue to support the market by additional injections of money, held by major investors (private investors, mutual funds, pension funds, hedge funds, investment banks), is reflected in high stock prices.

The positive impact of policy-maker support creates a Stock Market "Safety Net" that affects the price of shares. When we buy stocks, they are more expensive than they would be without the support of the policy makers. Most of the time, the prices of shares in the Stock Market are at their peak and most of the time do not reflect the condition of the real economy. There is a gap between the prices of stocks and the condition of the real economy.

In a Stock Market not supported by injections of money, current stock prices and values are based mainly on the predictions of profits that investors think the companies in the Stock Market will produce in the future.

In the NEW Stock Market, the investors know that, if necessary, policy makers (the Federal Reserve, US Treasury) will directly intervene and support the economy and the Stock Market, and if needed, even inject massive amounts of money.

**ZOOM-IN**
**_Investor mindset_**
_In the NEW Stock Market, investors believe in the existence of the Safety Net condition and the current prices of stocks reflect the investors' assumption that the Stock Market has built-in protection afforded by policy makers - in addition to the future expected profits of companies. Therefore, investors are ready to pay a higher price for stocks._

## The practical implication

The prices of stocks in the NEW Stock Market are more expensive, compared to a Stock Market not supported by injections of money.

The higher prices not only reflect the real value or future profits of the firms behind the stocks - they **also** reflect the investor assumption that there is a Safety Net in place, and that if needed, the policy makers will intervene in the Stock Market directly.

## Warning!

The securities and investment strategies mentioned in this book do not constitute suggestions, or any type of recommendation regarding what you should or should not invest in.

If you are not an experienced investor. It is highly recommended that you build and accompany your investment decisions with the help and guidance of a licensed financial advisor.

# How can the "Safety Net" condition impact Buying and Selling Decisions made by investors?

**Why does the "Safety Net" condition support the decision to <u>sell</u> once the price of stocks increases considerably (by at least 5 precent)?**

For example, if you invest in an ETF on the S&P, and there is a positive sentiment for the S&P index and it rises over 5 precent, then, because of its high prices (present even before the positive sentiment), the upward trend in prices will exhaust itself sooner than later.

If we invest our money in an ETF on the S&P **before** the prices go up and wait for it to rally, then we can cash in (sell our stocks). If we wait too long after the S&P has reached new peaks, we may face a decline in our investment.

# The common behavior of investors after a rally

### Natural price correction - investors cash in

After a considerable rally (at least 5 precent), some of the investors who bought the stocks before the rally decide to sell the stocks and materialize their profits.

### Low positive sentiment to good news (after a rally)

If there is further good news **after** a rally, the price of stocks will be positively impacted, **but** most likely to a mild degree only, because the prices of stocks had been high (the Safety Net assumption). Therefore, the additional positive news will only justify the high prices.

### High volatility to bad news (after a rally)

Because of the high prices, the volatility of the market to bad news is high. So, when bad news is published the reaction of the investors will be aggressive. The bad news will give the investors both a reason and the incentive to cash in.

## A deeper explanation

After a major rally in the Stock Market or in a specific sector, when additional good news appears, it only justifies the existence of the high prices that the stocks had already reached. Therefore, the effect on stock prices may be a slight positive impact - and there may even be no impact at all.

But if there is bad news (**after a major rally**), such as lower than expected firm profitability, this can raise doubt regarding the justification of the high prices and bring bad sentiment to the market. Therefore, there is a high probability that the stock prices will be impacted in a negative way. The investors will have greater motivation to materialize their profits.

## Final conclusion

After a considerable rally in stock prices, the sensitivity to bad news in the Stock Market or a specific sector is higher than the sensitivity to good news.

## Why does the "Safety Net" condition support the decision to <u>buy</u> after prices go down considerably (at least 5 precent)?

If prices go down considerably - there is a reason: it can be something that happened in the real economy, or in the financial markets.

For example, if unemployment is much higher than forecast, this economic data will negatively impact the stocks in sectors directly related to the real economy, such as banks for example.

If the negative trend continues, we as investors can predict that policy makers will act sometime in the foreseeable future and things will change for the better. We don't know exactly what specific action policy makers will take or when exactly it will happen, but we know that at some point in time in the foreseeable future, they will make a decision that will impact the economy and the market in a positive way.

Since this can take days, weeks, or even longer, we as investors can only wait until it happens.

### Low volatility to bad news (after prices fall)

After we purchase stocks during the waiting period (before they rise considerably) things also can worsen, but here is the paradox - there is an inverted relationship of policy makers to bad economic developments. If economic conditions worsen, the help from the policy makers will come sooner rather than later. You have a lifeline provided by the strongest economic entities in the world - the US Federal Reserve and the American Treasury.

## Final conclusion

After a considerable decline in stock prices the sensitivity of a specific sector or specific index in the Stock Market to bad news is less than the sensitivity to good news.

## Why does the condition that other alternatives are less attractive than the Stock Market, support the decision to Buy when prices have gone down considerably (at least 5 precent?)

When you buy an ETF after it goes down considerably (at least 5 precent), you can assume in advance that the investors selling their stocks don't have better alternatives.

As an investor, you can assume that there is a high probability that this money (that left the market due to the sale) will return, sooner rather than later, to the Stock Market.

When this money is reinvested into the Stock Market, it will create a positive impact on the prices of shares.

**BE AWARE!**

*It's important to note that we can buy and sell ETFs on stocks in parts. When we buy or sell in parts, we first have to decide, in advance, how much money we want to invest in an ETF, and then divide the sum of money into two parts.*

*For example, if the Nasdaq index drops five percept, we can use the first half of the money to purchase an ETF on the Nasdaq; and if the Nasdaq prices continue to drop another four percent (nine percent in total), we can also buy an ETF on the Nasdaq with the second half of the money. The same division into two parts can also be made when we sell the ETF.*

## How can the "quick positive sentiment rotation between sectors" impact investors' decisions?

In normal times, the rotation of positive sentiment between sectors can take an average three months. In the NEW Stock Market, the prices of stocks are high because of the "Safety Net" assumption. The rotation can take only weeks and sometimes even days.

**Why does this condition support the decision to BUY after a fall down (of at least 5 precent)?**

After a price fall in a sector (at least 5 precent you can assume that, due to the rotation assumption, investors will "rediscover" the sector in the foreseeable future, as its prices become more attractive compared to other sectors.

For example, if we see that the Nasdaq index falls considerably, and in the same time, stock prices in the banking sectors reach new heights, then it's only a matter of weeks (sometimes even days) until investors will feel that the banking sector has run its course and move to sectors with more attractive prices. It is likely (in this example) that some of the money will be reinvested in shares that belong to the Nasdaq.

**Why does this assumption/condition support the decision to SELL after a rise in shares prices (of at least 5 precent)?**

When investors see that the prices of certain indexes or sectors have reached peak levels and run their course, they have a tendency to materialize their profits and reinvest their money in another sector. They look for a sector whose prices are cheaper (more attractive) and whose value may rise.

151

## The practical implementation of the short-term investment strategy

When you, as an investor, see a leading sector (big banks) or an index (S&P, Nasdaq) being negatively impacted - i.e., its prices have gone down by **five percent or more** - then you can use an ETF to buy its stocks. **It's your decision** how much money to invest, if at all.

**BE AWARE!**
*The decision regarding the definition of a considerable downfall that justifies a decision to buy - is yours. In a stormy Stock Market with high volatility, the rule of at least a five percent drop may be appropriate. But in a less volatile Stock Market, the rule of thumb can be different. In a "quiet" market, the decision to consider buying an ETF on stocks even after a fall of only three percent, and not five percent, may be justified.*

You can decide to split your investment in the sector into two parts: the first, after the sector drops at least four percent, and the second, after it drops **at least** an additional three percent.

If the prices continue to fall, don't be tempted to buy more.

Wait until something positive impacts the stocks in the sector/index and its prices rise at least five precent relative to the price at which you purchased the stocks.

You never know when the positive sentiment will return. You never know what the specific reason for the positive impact will be.

After the sector/index you invested your money in is positively impacted, if the shares rise by at least five percent you can sell the ETF you bought and materialize your profits.

**BE AWARE!**

*The short-term investment strategy is supported by the existence of the three conditions. If you assume that all the three conditions exist, you can use the short-time strategy to profit from the NEW Stock Market.*

## What is the BIG advantage of using the strategy of buying low and selling high?

In an investment strategy based on buying when stock prices go down considerably and selling when prices go up considerably, you invest **without** any specific knowledge or information about what will happen in the future or when. You only assume that the three conditions exist.

*IN MY EXPERIENCE*
*Leading investing companies and hedge funds also use the short-term investment strategy.*

## NEW, previously unknown information vs. known information

In the Stock Market, the value of known information is considered to be near zero.

# Why?

There is always the assumption that the present prices of shares in the Stock Market already reflect future expectations.

Therefore, what moves the markets up or down is always new, unexpected information. We can clearly see this effect when economic data is released.

If, for example, the unemployment rate rises considerably higher **than was expected** by the investors in the market, we will see that stock prices are influenced in a negative way.

If the rate of unemployment is as expected, then this information in itself will probably not impact the Stock Market at all - given, of course, that other economic and financial factors behave as expected.

When we buy ETFs in a sector whose stock prices were falling considerably (by more than five percent), we assume that sometime in the foreseeable future something positive will happen in the economy or the firm's profitability (although we don't know when or what), and that this specific sector will experience positive sentiment that will lead to a rally of its stocks prices.

The amazing thing is that there is no certainty regarding this information when we buy the stocks, but the value of this information is high; and when the positive impact materializes, we can sell our stocks with a nice profit.

If it were the opposite, and this information were accompanied by a 100 percent certainty when we bought the securities, then when the expected good news would be received, our profits would be close to zero - because the prices of the stocks purchased already embodied the good news.

**ZOOM-IN**
*Investor mindset*
*If Stock Market investors know exactly when and what positive things are going to happen in a specific sector in advance, this will be reflected in the present, with higher stock prices. Therefore, when the good things actually happen, they won't impact the prices of stocks at all.*

## The main conclusion:

Paradoxically, our ability to profit as investors is increased when we buy stocks without knowing when they will rise again or what exactly will impact them. In a sense, we can say that we are also buying uncertainty. When we buy, we assume that something good will happen in the foreseeable future. We don't know when or what, and neither do the other investors in the market.

In the Stock Market, the value of unknown information is considered to be the most valuable information.

## Conclusions concerning your investment decisions

### IN: NEW Stock Market

**Buy Low, Sell High**

When share prices in a major index or a sector **go down** considerably (by at least five percent), it's time to consider using an ETF to buy these stocks.

When share prices in a major index or a sector **go up** considerably (by at least five percent), it's time to consider selling the index or ETF and materializing your profits.

**Invest in the NEW Stock Market based on unknown information**

Investment decisions that are based on previously unknown and unexpected information have much higher value in the Stock Market than those based on known information, which is already reflected in the prices of stocks.

### OUT: OLD Stock Market

Fundamental analysis of stocks.

# Epilogue

**REMEMBER:**

You won't get any prizes just
for knowing things.
You'll only be rewarded for your actions
You gained valuable information -
Use it!

If this book helps you better understand

the NEW Stock Market,

I would highly appreciate your review on Amazon.

Thank you in advance,

Jacob Nayman

# A brief summary
# of
# the book

OLD Stock Market
## OUT
NEW Stock Market
## IN

# Chapter 1

## IN: NEW Stock Market

### The Golden Rule of the senior investment advisor

Buy stocks (using an ETF) when their prices drop considerably.

Sell the stocks (the ETF) when their prices rise considerably.

## OUT: OLD Stock Market

Long-term investing.

# Chapter 2

## IN: NEW Stock Market

### The NEW Stock Market matrix

#### The price of a stock reflects:

The "Safety Net" assumption.

The "Lack of Attractive Alternatives" assumption.

The "Rapid Rotation Between Sectors" assumption.

### FOMO: The Fear of Missing Out

As investors, we can wait for the economy to heal completely, and only then invest our money in the Stock Market. However, it may take years until the economy is 100 percent healthy. Most investors won't wait because of the fear of missing out.

## OUT: OLD Stock Market

The price of a stock reflects a company's current value and it also reflects the prospects for a company, the growth that investors expect of it in the future.

# Chapter 3

## IN: NEW Stock Market

### The risky part of investments

Short-term profits - using ETFs

### Equity diversification

Invest some of the money in foreign Stock Markets

### Currency diversification

Invest in leading currencies other than the US dollar - such as the euro, Swiss franc, etc.

### The solid part of investments

Gold, crude oil, linked bonds

Equity and currency diversification

High liquidity (cash and equivalents)

# Chapter 4

## IN: NEW Stock Market

### The Policy makers control the market

A Stock Market that is supported by trillions of dollars injected into the economy and the financial markets and totally controlled by policy makers. Policy makers' decisions and the injections of money create a kind of a Safety Net in the Stock Market.

### Short-term profits

The massive injections of money and the fluctuations in the prices of shares in the NEW Stock Market create opportunities for investors to enjoy short-term profits.

### The NEW economic matrix

The first two scenarios in the economic matrix support the existence of the three conditions. The third scenario - the doomsday scenario - doesn't support the three conditions.

## OUT: OLD Stock Market

### The real economic fundamentals are in good shape

The interventions by policy-makers are minimal. In most cases, the prices of shares reflect the conditions in the real economy.

### Long-term investments

We, or our financial advisors, buy stocks that are considered to be good investments in the long run. After holding the stocks for several years, we sell them and can enjoy a nice profit.

# Chapter 5

### IN: NEW Stock Market

### Printing money

The monetary easing used by the Federal Reserve (central bank) in the financial markets, and fiscal policy - that is implemented by the US Treasury in the real economy.

### Policy makers

Intervention in the economy and in the markets. The main policy involves the injection of trillions of dollars to the economy and to financial markets. This creates a NEW Stock Market, with a new financial matrix.

### OUT: OLD Stock Market

### Lowering interest rates

Used in the past to fight recession,
this strategy has become less relevant.

### Free economic forces

The prices in the Stock Market reflect the economy and the profitability of firms.

# Chapter 6

### IN: NEW Stock Market

### Overweighting winning sectors

Deliver alpha (an excess return over the S&P) by overweighting winning sectors and underweighting losers.

### Minimizing risk

Using ETFs to buy stocks in order to diversify.

### Taking advantage of the injections of money

Use of ETFs to benefit from the injections of money made by policy makers.

### OUT: OLD Stock Market

### Picking long-term stocks

The economic matrix shows us that there are inherent risks in long-term investments.

# Chapter 7

### IN: NEW Stock Market

### Cyclical Trends

If we want to take advantage of the policy makers' money injections we have to concentrate on short-term cyclical trends of sectors. The preferred time to buy is when the trend of the stock prices of a sector goes down. We assume that in the foreseeable future, something good will happen. We don't know precisely why and when it happens. However, when it happens, we will sell our stocks and enjoy a profit.

### OUT: OLD Stock Market

### Secular Trends

Because of the money injections, we can face inflation or, even worse, stagflation
(high inflation + recession). Investing in long-term stocks can turn out to be a wrong decision.

# Chapter 8

## IN: NEW Stock Market

### Deglobalization

A world economic environment with less cooperation between countries, decreased growth, and an increase in inflation pressures.

## OUT: OLD Stock Market

### Globalization

A global economic environment with high cooperation between countries, increased growth, and a reduction in inflation pressures.

# Chapter 9

## IN: NEW Stock Market

### The genie of inflation

Injections of money into the economy do not resolve the problem of the shrinking GDP. Therefore, although consumers preserve (in most cases) their buying power, fewer products and services are available. This can lead to increases in the prices of goods and services and the genie of inflation may appear.

## OUT: OLD Stock Market

### The dollar as a safe haven

Because printing large amounts of money and due to other

competing currencies around the world, the status of the US dollar as a reserve currency is in question. However, US policy makers will use any means in their economic arsenal to preserve the US dollar's status as the leading reserve currency in the world.

# Chapter 10

## IN: NEW Stock Market

### "U-shaped" (slow economic) recovery

The meaning of a U-shaped economic recovery is that the recession in the real economy is not going to disappear soon. This implies that the policy makers will continue to print money for years to come. In the context of our investments, the monetary policy, which provides super accommodative support of the Federal Reserve in the financial markets, will continue with the important ramifications of this policy on the prices of the equity markets. The high volatility of prices in the Stock Market will serve the short-time investment strategy.

## OUT: OLD Stock Market

### "V-shaped" (quick economic) recovery

If we believe that the economic recovery is going to be a V-shape, then we must assume that the injection of money into the economy and the financial markets is going to stop or decrease considerably. Thus, the volatility of the market will be reduced.

# Chapter 11

## *IN: NEW Stock Market*

### Short-term profits

Take advantage of the fluctuations in the NEW Stock Market by implementing the short-term investment strategy.

### High liquidity

Hold large amounts of cash and its equivalent to be prepared for any scenario.

## *OUT: OLD Stock Market*

### Long-term investments

In the long-run, there are three negative possibilities - inflation, recession and stagflation.

# Chapter 12

## *IN: NEW Stock Market*

### Short-term profit strategy

Buy stocks (using an ETF) when their prices drop considerably

Sell the stocks (the ETF) when their prices rise considerably

## *OUT: OLD Stock Market*

### Long-term investments.

# Chapter 13

## *IN: NEW Stock Market Buy Low, Sell High*

When share prices in a major index or a sector **go down** considerably (by at least five percent), it's time to consider using an ETF to buy these stocks.

When share prices in a major index or a sector **go up** considerably (by at least five percent), it's time to consider selling the index or ETF and materializing your profits.

### Invest in the NEW Stock Market based on unknown information

Investment decisions that are based on previously unknown and unexpected information have much higher value in the Stock Market than those based on known information, which is already reflected in the prices of stocks.

## *OUT: OLD Stock Market*

Fundamental analysis of stocks.

# A brief summary
## of
## the book

The 1%

# The 1st practice of the 1%

## Creating an income-generating investment portfolio

Having a good income is not always enough to secure our economic future. In order to maintain a reasonable standard of living over time, we need to generate a satisfactory income stream. One practical way to generate this additional income is to manage our finances in an optimal manner. We can do this by creating and managing a private investment portfolio.

This portfolio will enable us to generate additional revenues of thousands of dollars and more each year, from our savings. These revenues will give you the ability to maintain a standard of living that suits your present and future needs.

# The 2ⁿᵈ practice of the 1%

# BENCHMARKING

## Making optimal investment decisions using financial tools

When you need to make a decision whether to buy a financial product or keep a product in your private investment portfolio, it is recommended to use the Sharpe index. Using this simple but powerful benchmark tool will protect you from purchasing inferior financial products and give you the ability to choose the best investment products.

The Sharpe ratio is a tool for the calculation of risk-adjusted return. The Sharpe ratio can help explain whether a mutual fund that is managed by an investment company and has returns in excess of the benchmark is backed by smart investment decisions (made by the investment manager) or is the result of taking too much risk.

A higher Sharpe ratio indicates better performance of the investment manager or mutual fund.

# The 3<sup>rd</sup> practice of the 1%

## Create the optimal environment for your investment portfolio

Your private portfolio can be managed via several platforms: a bank, an investment company, or a brokerage firm.

It is important to make sure that the fees related to the management of your private investment portfolio are minimal. If you fail to do so, then the commissions you pay for your financial activity while managing your investment portfolio will generate nice profits for your bank or investment company - and your profitability as an investor will be low.

Even if you are used to working alone, you can still use some of the services offered by an investment advisor. The advantages of consulting with an advisor lie not only in the advice he can give you, but also in his access to central, sophisticated sources of information.

# The 4ᵗʰ practice of the 1%

**Using core-satellite asset allocation strategy**

Core-satellite investing strategy is a powerful method for asset allocation. You can decide to use this strategy to build your private investment portfolio.

## What is asset allocation?

Asset allocation is the implementation of an investment strategy in an investment portfolio.

The strategy attempts to balance risk versus reward by adjusting the percentage of each asset in your investment portfolio according to your personal preferences, the market conditions, and the economic environment.

## Core-satellite asset allocation

Core-satellite allocation strategy defines a "core" strategic element that comprises the most significant portion of the portfolio, and applies a dynamic "satellite" strategy to a smaller part of the portfolio. The "core" portion of the portfolio incorporates passive investments that don't require dynamic handling (i.e., index funds, exchange-traded funds (ETFs), mutual passive funds) while the "satellite" portion of the portfolio is composed of investments that demand a more dynamic approach. The expectation is that the satellite portion of your portfolio will outperform the market benchmark.

# The 5<sup>th</sup> practice of the 1%

## Build your risky investments as an independent entity

**There are two advantages to building the risky part of your investment portfolio separately from the solid part:**

First, the technical management of the portfolio is simplified and therefore easier to understand. Second, it's easier to measure the performance of the portfolio against market benchmarks: the risky part is compared to the performance of the Stock Market and high-yield bonds, and the solid part is compared to the benchmark of solid bonds.

**The satellite investments should outperform the benchmark of the "market portfolio."**

The satellite portion consists of active investments that are considerably more expensive than the passive investments.

The only justification for the higher price to be paid when investing in actively managed mutual fund investments is the assumption that the portfolio managers of such funds will manage the investments so that the overall returns of the entire portfolio beat the market benchmark. If not, then all of the money would be better invested in passive mutual funds or indexes.

# The 6th practice of the 1%

**Build your solid investments as an independent entity**

### The volatility of the financial markets

When the financial markets are in flux (inflation, currency fluctuations, interest rate changes, etc.): in such circumstances, you must know how to respond effectively to the changing market conditions. An investor who does not respond appropriately may suffer significant losses.

### The composition of the core creates two key advantages:

### *Minimized costs and minimized risk/volatility*

The first advantage is that the "core" is made up of passively managed securities, and the managing fees charged by portfolio managers, as well as the transaction costs, are considerably less expensive than for active investments.

The second advantage is that the "core" is composed of investments (index funds, ETFs, passive mutual funds) that approximately represent the "market portfolio"; therefore, there is a close to optimal diversification of the portfolio. The diversification ensures reduced volatility, meaning the overall risk of the investment portfolio is reduced.

# The 7ᵗʰ practice of the 1%

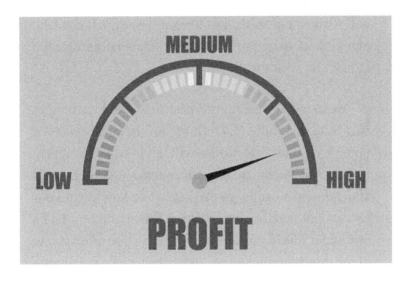

## Choosing and using the best funds and ETFs

Basically, your personal investment portfolio can be constructed by selecting individual securities. This will require a great deal of time and energy: it can take many years to acquire sufficient financial knowledge in just one sector or field.

Choosing and using the best funds and exchange-traded funds (ETFs) as an integral part of your investment portfolio will give you the ability to concentrate on making decisions regarding asset allocation in a changing market, while looking at your investment portfolio as a whole. When you buy ETFs or mutual funds, choose them wisely. Use at least one of the three parameters of cost, benchmark, and Sharpe ratio. The end result will be that out of the thousands of mutual funds offered in the financial market, your investment portfolio will contain the ones with the best performance.

# The 8ᵗʰ practice of the 1%

## Profit from the expertise of financial institutions

The portfolio managers of various financial institutions have professional knowledge and expertise that you can profit from. However, at the same time, they also have several significant limitations. When managing your own private investment portfolio, you need to know how to benefit from their advantages (such as the purchase of excellent, leading mutual funds for your private portfolio), while remaining well aware of their limitations. You - and you alone - are responsible for counteracting those limitations; and if you do so - then you will earn significantly more on your money.

### Disabling the constraints and profiting from the opportunities

As noted, the investment managers at financial institutions have limitations that may lead them to operate contrary to their professional judgment. But these restrictions are not applicable to you: you can always sell the fund/ETF.

You, and only you, have the responsibility to get rid of the fund/ETF or reduce your exposure to risk, thus reducing the damage that may be caused to your money.

For example, in good times you should increase your exposure to funds/ETF shares, and in challenging times you should reduce exposure and move to more conservative funds. When the market reaches low price levels, indicating, among others things, the panic in the general public, you can take advantage of the situation and buy funds/ETFs to collect stocks at attractive prices.

# The 9<sup>th</sup> practice of the 1%

## Avoiding exotic financial products

There are thousands of companies and individuals around the world who offer financial solutions for making easy money. In most cases, they are registered in, and operate from, countries with no financial regulation.

Basically, their only goal is to take your money. They know how to accurately identify your financial goals and needs, and they will do anything to move your money from your bank account to their pocket. Their only real expertise is in the psychology of people.

Dealing with forex trading or binary options trading involves a double risk: the first stems from the very nature of the investments, which themselves are dangerous.

The second is the fact that in most cases, these financial products are under no regulation, so the companies that try to sell us these financial products can manipulate you any way they choose. Overall, it isn't wise to invest your money in them.

In contrast, structured products can be used as an alternative to a direct investment, as part of the asset allocation strategy to reduce the risk exposure of your portfolio.

But you have to be very cautious when you buy them: even if you decide to invest in them, do so only when the entity behind the product is a regulated company, such as a bank or a large investment company, and only invest a relatively small amount of money - in the range of several thousand dollars per structure. If it is difficult for you to understand the payoff features of the structured product and its risk characteristics - then don't buy it in the first place.

# The 10th practice of the 1%

## Understanding and using leading market indicators

There are a number of leading financial indicators that influence the interest rates and therefore your investment portfolio. These include the consumer price index (CPI), gross domestic product (GDP), housing starts, joblessness claims, and durable goods orders.

The indicators presented here all have a common denominator: they must be analyzed over a period of time, so the direction of their trend is revealed. When you analyze them over time, it is particularly important to check how an increase or decrease in specific indicators impacts inflationary pressures and hence causes an increase or decrease in interest rates.

This information can be used as a powerful tool for the optimal management of your investment portfolio.

### Interest rates and your investment portfolio

When deciding where to invest your money, you have several alternatives. If you know that the solid channel offers you a high interest rate with only a very low risk, then you presumably will put most of your money in solid investments, such as government bonds. In such circumstances your motivation to put money into risky investments, such as stocks, will be low, and your level of exposure to risky assets will drop.

The opposite is also true: the lower the interest rates are, the more willing you will be prepared to take more risks in order to generate higher returns, and the higher your level of exposure to risky assets will be.

# A brief summary
# of
# the book

**GOLDEN MONEY TIPS**

# Golden Tip #1

**The most effective way to receive benefits from your bank**

### *The ultimatum tactic*

If you want to achieve significantly improved terms for your banking operations, the best thing you can do is tell the bank what you've been offered by a competitor bank.

You can't be vague: you must specify the name of the competing bank and the exact benefits or exemptions they've offered you. Along with your request for additional benefits, you can add the threat, either implicit or explicit, that if they can't meet their competitor's offer, then your money and income will be transferred to the other bank.

If you are vague and have nothing to back up your threat/request, then your bank won't take you seriously.

# Golden Tip #2

## Play it safe - diversify: get higher rewards with minimal risk

### Why invest in something if you know that it's riskier?

The only situation in which you should be willing to tolerate higher risk is one in which you expect to be rewarded with higher profits.

"Don't put all your eggs in one basket" is the golden rule. If you violate this rule, you risk losing your investments with no higher probability of returns. Studies show that portfolio investment in at least 20 securities will achieve adequate diversification. In addition to, or instead of diversification, you can buy ETFs or mutual funds. By their very nature, ETFs and mutual funds are less risky because they spread their investment across many securities.

# Golden Tip #3

## Risk management as an instrument that protects our money

From a holistic perspective, the protection afforded by insurance coverage can be considered a risk management tool. These particular tools protect our assets, financial and physical, accumulated over years of hard work.

If you and/or your family members find yourselves in any type of negative situation (work disability, disease, disability, the need for long-term care or death) without the protection afforded by insurance coverage, the standard of living to which you are accustomed can be severely reduced, since you will be forced to bear the financial burden - and not the insurance company.

The general premise of insurance is that you, as a customer, are buying peace of mind - while the insurance company buys your risk.

# Golden Tip #4

**Make money, not percentages**

The less risky the investment, the more confidence you can have in allowing yourself to invest larger sums of money. Even if the percentage you earn is smaller than the percentage offered by speculative investments, the total sum of the profit will be significantly greater. Therefore, knowing how to invest in low-risk investments is important - often even more so than having detailed knowledge of speculative investments.

# Golden Tip #5

## How can you identify the best mutual funds?

## "All or nothing" strategy

An investment company takes significantly more risk than its competitors. If the company succeeds, it will win public appreciation, and the end result will be that more investors, having seen the "success" of the company, will buy its mutual funds. The investors are unaware of the fact that to achieve these "attractive" results, the company took big risks with their investors' money. If the company fails, however, their investors will suffer the damage.

The only way to protect yourself from the "all or nothing" strategy is to look at the company's long-range performance. Don't decide to invest your money in an investment company's mutual fund based purely on its short-term performance results. Base your decision on its performance over the last three to five years.

# Golden Tip #6

**Sometimes it's best to just "sit it out"**

When the Stock Market weakens, or when there are indications that it will fall, there are many financial institutions that will try to encourage you to stay in the market. Why? Because they profit from the commissions you pay them. Never just blindly follow their advice - make sure to analyze the situation and determine what is best for your finances.

If you know that you can't leave your money invested for at least two years, then it is better not to invest it in stocks at all. In bad economic times, don't just passively leave your money invested for the long term. In some situations, it's a good idea to withdraw some or all of your investments to safeguard against significant future losses; in other situations, it's better to "sit it out " and wait for better days.

# Golden Tip #7

## "Pay to Play": The Stock Market's cover charge

We all know that we should buy stocks at a "cheap" price and sell them at a "high" price. The problem is identifying the two points at the ends of the spectrum - the minimum and the maximum value of the stock.

One way to estimate the best time to buy or sell is to rely on speculation based on futuristic economic analysis of the Stock Market. Another way is to wait for the market to "speak" - to show signs of life. In this method, you purchase stocks at a higher price only after the market shows larger trading volumes and positive macroeconomic data.

The difference between the price you could have paid for the stocks at the start of the rise and the higher price you pay later is the cover charge - the "entry premium." This "entry premium" is worth its cost, because by waiting, you invest your money in a market that shows concrete signs that the timing of your investment is right.

# Golden Tip #8

## How to use mutual funds and ETFs as tools to manage your money

As an investor who manages his own personal investment portfolio, you should decide during which periods of time to invest in mutual funds/ETFs. You can think of mutual funds or ETFs like a train running along the market's trend line (i.e., the "tracks"). You, the investor in these funds/ETFs, are not the train driver, but a passenger who can choose when to stay on the train and when to get off; in addition to buying and selling, you can also decide how much money to invest.

If you think the market is doing well, increase your exposure to risky assets by purchasing riskier funds/ETFs. When you see that the market is coming close to peaking and the market is saturated, you can decide to minimize your exposure to risk by moving your money to less risky investments, namely solid mutual funds or ETFs.

# Golden Tip #9

## How to avoid the 5 pitfalls of portfolio management

## Pitfall #1

In all of the cases in which investors were robbed of their money, their biggest mistake was their decision to transfer money to an account not registered in their name. If a licensed portfolio manager wants to manage your money, he should do so from an account that is in your name only.

## Pitfall #2

If a portfolio manager doesn't "bother" you with a lot of questions - only promises that you will get a high return on your money, without any risk, then your money is in great danger.

## Pitfall #3

If the investment company takes commissions on the purchase and sale of the securities, then the additional fees you pay should be minimal, and the number of selling and buying operations should be reasonable. If this is not the case, then the cost of operating your portfolio will be so high that your odds of making a

214

profit will be low. The only one who will profit from your portfolio will be the investment company.

## Pitfall #4

In some cases, the portfolio manager may not have enough experience, and because he wants to get results "no matter what the price" he may choose to take unnecessary risks, endangering your money. It's a bit like choosing a doctor - find one who has extensive experience and a good record.

## Pitfall #5

The biggest commissions of investment companies come from their top customers, so in most cases they will do almost anything to retain them as investors-even at the expense of their regular customers. One of the best ways to protect yourself from such companies is to do an online background check - a simple internet research - to see if their names come up, before you invest with them.

# Golden Tip #10

**Balancing your investment portfolio**

Balancing your portfolio means buying and selling securities in a way that will return the portfolio to its desired risk levels. They do not have to be the same risk levels you chose when you first built the portfolio.

Decisions related to changing the proportions of the risky/solid portions of your portfolio should be based on present macroeconomic data and your own, personal risk preferences. Keep in mind that if you gain relatively large returns on your portfolio, you might prefer to have greater exposure to stocks. You may be able to take more risk, since after all, even if the market were to drop, you would probably only lose money you already earned as a profit (and not your original investment sum). And of course, always remember that greater risk can lead to higher profits.

# Glossary

## A

### Active investor

An investor who uses his knowledge to invest money saved by underspending in a private investment portfolio. The portfolio is built in a manner that enables him to minimize costs and volatility and provides him with an opportunity to outperform the market benchmark.

### All or nothing strategy

The basic idea behind the "all or nothing" strategy is that the investment company takes significantly more risk than its competitors. As a result, it can produce significantly higher profits. Investors are usually not aware that to achieve these "attractive" results, the company took significant risks with their money.

### Asset allocation

Asset allocation is the implementation of an investment strategy in an investment portfolio. The strategy attempts to balance between risk and reward by adjusting the percentage of each asset in the investment portfolio according to the customer's personal preferences, the market conditions and the economic environment. The main assumption in asset allocation is that investment in different assets results in portfolio diversification, which reduces the overall risk in the customer investment portfolio while maintaining the expected return level.

### Average life of a bond

The average duration, in annual terms, of the bond. The longer the term, the riskier the bond.

# B

### Balancing an investment portfolio

Balancing your portfolio means buying and selling securities in a way that will return the portfolio to its desired risk levels. They do not have to be the same risk levels you chose when you first built the portfolio.

## Benchmark

A benchmark is a standard against which the performance of a mutual fund or the performance of an investment manager can be measured. When evaluating the performance of any investment, it's important to compare it against an appropriate benchmark. For example, to evaluate the performance of your investment manager or your private investment portfolio you can use the S&P 500, the Dow Jones Industrial Average, or the Russell 2000 Index.

## Binary options

A binary option is a financial option in which the payoff is either a defined, fixed monetary amount - or nothing at all. Binary options are used in a theoretical framework as the building block for asset pricing and financial derivatives.

## Bonds

A loan you give the government or a company. When you hold bonds, you have a chance of receiving the "guaranteed return" even if the company suffers financial difficulties or bankruptcy; the company shareholders, in contrast, can lose all of their money.

## Bond rating

A rating which indicates the probability that the borrower (the government / corporation) will meet their obligations and return the invested money + the promised interest. Corporate bonds are rated according to their level of risk. The rating is given by professional companies that specialize in this area. The rating provides investors with information regarding the risk of investing in the various bonds. If the rating of a bond is low, it means that the risk - the probability that you could lose all your money - is high.

# C

## Central bank

A central bank is an institution that manages a country's currency, money supply, and interest rates; and uses monetary policy to achieve the objectives of the government. The responsibilities of the central bank include controlling and managing interest rates, setting the reserve requirement, and during times of financial crisis, helping the banking sector to function properly. In most countries, central banks also monitor and supervise financial institutions (including banks) to reduce the risk of reckless or fraudulent activities.

### Company shares

Unlike bonds, shares have no "guaranteed return." In other words, they do not guarantee a predictable cash flow to be paid on a specified future date. When you hold shares, you rely on their market value.

### Consumer Price Index

The consumer price index (CPI) measures change in the price of a market basket of consumer goods and services purchased by households. Changes in the CPI are used as measures of inflation.

### Core-satellite allocation strategy

Core-satellite allocation strategy defines a "core" strategic element that comprises the most significant portion of the portfolio, and applies a dynamic "satellite" strategy to the smaller part of the portfolio. The "core" portion of the portfolio incorporates passive investments that don't require dynamic handling (i.e. index funds, exchange-traded funds (ETFs), mutual passive funds), while the "satellite" portion of the portfolio is composed of investments that demand a more dynamic approach. In the satellite portion, the portfolio is adjusted to include the assets, sectors, or individual stocks that show the most potential for gains. The expectation is that the satellite portion of the portfolio will outperform the market benchmark.

# D

## Diversification

"Don't put all your eggs in one basket" is the golden rule. If this rule is not adhered to, there is a risk that the investments will be lost, with no higher probability of returns. Studies have shown that investing in over 20 securities can eliminate the specific risk of an investment portfolio: the only risk that will remain is the market risk. Diversification enables maximum returns with minimum risk.

## Durable goods orders

An economic indicator that reflects the number of new orders placed with domestic manufacturers for the delivery of factory hard goods (in the near term or in the future).

# E

## Entry premium

The difference between the price you could have paid for the stocks at the start of the rise in the Stock

Market and the higher price you pay later is called the cover charge, or "entry premium."

## ETF

An ETF (exchange traded fund) is a marketable security that tracks an index, a commodity, bonds or a basket of assets. Like a mutual fund, an ETF is a pool of investments; however, an ETF will often have lower associated costs. Unlike mutual funds, an ETF trades like a common stock on the stock exchange, and its price changes throughout the day as it is bought and sold.

## Exotic financial products

Unregulated financial products that contain a lot of false promises. There are financial products that are difficult to understand, introduced as "sexy" and profitable, which are indeed composed of elements that are very profitable - but only to the seller. If you give into temptation and buy them, they can hurt the returns in your investment portfolio.

## Exposure to foreign currencies

If you buy a financial product traded in a foreign country, in most cases it will be influenced by the currency exchange of that country. Therefore, buying

ETFs on overseas stock indexes, for example, exposes you to foreign currency fluctuations.

# F
## Fees for securities

The level of commission for buying and selling securities and financial products is very important for your financial activity.

## Financial freedom

The ability to produce a steady income and maintain your desired lifestyle even when you don't work.

## Financial advisor

The advisor has access to reports prepared by the Economics Department of the financial institution at which they are employed. These reports can provide essential information on the basis of which, among other things, it can be determined how much foreign currency you should keep in your investment portfolio; and on the basis of which an institutional recommendation can be made regarding the percent to invest in various investment channels.

### Financial platforms

A bank, an investment company, or a brokerage firm.

### Financial simulators

Used to simulate asset allocations based on customer preferences while taking the macroeconomic conditions in the market into account.

### Forex

The Foreign Exchange global market, where currencies are traded. It is decentralized, meaning there is no central marketplace for foreign exchange; instead, currency trading is conducted electronically, "over the counter" (OTC) - all transactions between traders around the world occur via computer networks. The market is open 24 hours a day except on weekends. The foreign exchange market assists international trade and business by providing a platform for currency conversion.

### Future market expectations

If the market expects that the central bank will raise interest rates in the near future, the market will not "wait" until it actually happens - it will react as if the increase in interest rates has already been implemented.

# G
## *GDP*

The gross domestic product (GDP) is a measure of the total market value of all final goods and services produced in a period (quarterly or yearly).

## *Government Bonds*

Always safer than corporate bonds: the government can always print more money to meet its obligations, while companies depend on their financial strength to meet their obligations.

# H
## *Housing starts*

Housing starts reflect the number of new, privately-owned houses on which construction has been started in a given period.

# I
## *Interest rates*

When deciding where to invest your money, you have several alternatives. The solid channel offers investments with only a very low risk; therefore, if interest rates are high, it is preferable to put most of your money in solid investments, such as government bonds.

In such circumstances your investments will enjoy high interest rates, and your level of exposure to risky assets will drop. The opposite is also true: the lower the interest rates are, the more worthwhile it is to take risks in order to generate higher returns; the level of exposure to risky assets, such as stocks, will usually be higher. When interest rates are low the demand for risky assets is higher, and the prices, accordingly, are also higher.

### Investment company

An investment company is a corporation or a trust that invests the money of investors in financial securities.

### Insurance premiums

An insurance premium is the amount of money an individual or business pays for an insurance policy.

### Investment horizon

The longer the investment horizon, the higher the level of risk you can afford to be exposed to, since your investments will have plenty of time to ride out the market's short-term fluctuations. Accordingly, the potential to gain higher returns will be greater.

## Investor preferences

The portfolio should be built in accordance with investor desires and needs; to accomplish this, the following issues should be addressed: the sum of money to be invested in the private portfolio, the period of the investment, and exposure to risk and the required return.

## J

### Joblessness claims

This report tracks how many new people filed for unemployment benefits in the previous week.

## L

### Leading market indicators

An active government has several important economic obligations / objectives that it should actively pursue: high employment, price stability, and economic growth.

### Liquidity

Liquidity refers to the portion of the portfolio that you can immediately realize to cash without incurring a loss in returns. Although you receive very low returns from the liquid portion, it's an important part of the overall investment portfolio. The liquidity allows you to act quickly if there are opportunities in the financial market. If you need a high level of liquidity, then cash and cash equivalents can meet this requirement.

# M

## Market benchmarks

The risky part of the investment is compared to the performance of the Stock Market and high-yield bonds, and the solid part is compared to the benchmark of solid bonds.

## "Market portfolio"

A theoretical concept. It is defined as a portfolio consisting of investments that include every financial asset available in the world market. The representation of each asset in the "market portfolio" is proportional to its total presence in the world market. Because its components mirror all of the assets in the financial world, the expected return of the market portfolio should be identical to the expected return of the whole market. Since the market portfolio, by definition, is optimally diversified, it is subject only to risks that affect the whole market, and not to the risks relevant to a particular asset in the portfolio. In the process of building an investment portfolio based on the "market portfolio" concept, investors use proxies for the market portfolio such as the S&P 500 in the US, the FTSE 100 in the UK, the DAX in Germany, and more.

## Market volatility

Can be expressed by inflation, deflation, fluctuations in interest rates, currencies and the Stock Market.

## Mutual funds

A pool of money from many investors used to purchase securities, which include stocks, bonds, money market instruments and similar assets. In essence, mutual funds are joint investments. When you invest your money in them, they allow you to use licensed portfolio managers to manage your investment and thereby benefit from their knowledge and experience.

## Market risk of a security

The product of macroeconomic factors, such as a sharp rise in interest rates, inflation, deflation, a crisis in a major market player (Europe, the United States, or China), and more.

## Marketability

The ease with which you can buy and sell securities at market price when you choose to do so.

## Monetary policy

In the United States, the Federal Reserve is in charge of the monetary policy. The Federal Reserve has 4 main economic goals: to achieve maximum employment (close to 95%); to maintain stable prices (2-3% inflation per year); to keep interest rates relatively low; and to provide banks with liquidity that enables them to operate in a "healthy" way. To achieve all 4 goals the Federal Reserve uses a monetary policy, which is implemented through the actions of the central bank. The main "weapon" used by the Federal Reserve is the control, and if needed, adjustment of the interest rate. It does this by financial actions such as buying or selling government bonds and changing the amount of money that banks are required to keep in their reserves. These actions have far-reaching implications for the economy, as they impact the interest rates on savings accounts, corporate bonds, student loans and mortgages.

# P

### Portfolio manager

Portfolio managers make investment decisions for a fund or group of funds under their control. They base their investment decisions on their evaluation of the financial markets. They buy and sell securities as the conditions in the Stock Market changes.

# R
## *Regulated financial product*

A regulated financial product must meet three basic conditions:

1. It must be sold by a licensed financial entity, preferably a financial institution (a bank, an investment company), that operates in the country you live in;
2. The money to purchase the product must remain in a bank account registered in your name, i.e. there is no demand that you transfer your money to another account; and
3. The product is simple and easy to understand.

## *Risk vs. return relationship*

Higher returns on investments - higher profits - require more risk.

# S
## *Satellite portion of an investment portfolio*

The dynamic element - The satellite portion will be built from actively managed investments. These are investments that do not reflect the "market portfolio."

The goal: The expected returns should outperform the returns of the "market portfolio."

## Specific security risk

Derives from specific negative events such as strikes, mismanagement, embezzlement, or risk that decreases the company's profit due to an unexpected event. This type of risk may lead to a sharp drop in the price of the company's shares.

## Sharpe ratio

The Sharpe ratio is a tool for the calculation of risk-adjusted return. The Sharpe ratio can help explain whether a portfolio or investment company that has returns in excess of the benchmark is backed by smart investment decisions or is the result of taking too much risk. A higher Sharpe ratio indicates better performance of the investment manager.

## Spot market

The place where currencies are bought and sold according to the current price. The current price is a reflection of many variables. The forwards and the futures markets are used by international corporations to protect themselves against future fluctuations in exchange rates.

## Solid bonds

All of the bonds in the solid investment part of the portfolio should meet two criteria: first, the bonds should have an average maturity of up to 5 years or less. Second, the corporate bonds should have high ratings (AA or higher). Bonds that do not meet those criteria are not considered solid investments.

## Structured product

Also known as a market-linked investment, a structured product is created through a process of financial engineering. It is a pre-packaged investment strategy based on a combination of underlying factors such as shares, bonds, indices or commodities with derivatives (like options, forwards, and swaps).

# T

### Transparency

The investment company that sells the financial product is required by law to publish a prospectus before beginning its operations. A prospectus is a document that contains important details for investors, such as specifics regarding investment policies.

# U

## *Ultimatum tactic*

"I've been given an offer by your competitor. If you can't match it or better, I will transfer my money to him."

# V

## *VIX*

The CBOE Volatility Index, known by its ticker symbol VIX, is a popular measure of the Stock Market's expectation of volatility implied by S&P 500 index options. It is calculated and published on a real-time basis by the Chicago Board Options Exchange (CBOE), and is commonly referred to as the "fear index" or the "fear gauge."

# Y

## *Yield to maturity*

The annual return of the investor, if the bond is held until its maturity.

# Z

## *Zero sum game*

An economic concept according to which one investor's gains must be balanced by another investor's losses.

# What next?

*Enjoyed reading the current book?*
*Have you already read The 1%?*

Made in the USA
Las Vegas, NV
19 August 2021

28472684R00134